THE
CUSTOMER
EXPERIENCE
FIASCO

THE
CUSTOMER
EXPERIENCE
FIASCO

Navigating the Pitfalls of a

Customer Experience Strategy...

ANDREW REISE CONSULTING

Book Design by AuthorSupport.com

ISBN 978-0-5780-8910-2 (Soft Cover)
ISBN 978-0-9889685-0-9 (Hard Cover)

ABOUT
THE AUTHORS

Consultants, husbands, fathers, and friends; these are just a few roles we play. We've spent our careers helping clients understand and strengthen their customer relationships.

We built Andrew Reise Consulting on the premise that there is a better way to deliver value to the customer. We don't want to just improve the experience, but align the appropriate experience to the company's goals and mission. We wanted to share our beliefs and approach, so we wrote this book.

When we are not helping clients, we're typically somewhere in the Midwest, golfing, biking, fishing, running, playing football, or spending time with family and friends around the BBQ.

Pictured from Left to Right

Jeff Lewandowski, Josh Hilgers, Nathan Haskins,
Rob Howard, Ken Tomlen, Tim Carrigan,
Dan Arthur, Andy Mattox

Scott Stamper (Not Pictured)

SPECIAL THANKS

To Our Clients:

For providing us an opportunity to serve you and your companies in the best way we know how. You have trusted us to deliver with your most vital business initiatives and continue to believe in us. Together we have built true partnerships which extend beyond the inherent business goals. Thank you for allowing us to do what we love.

To all the Consultants at Andrew Reise Consulting:

For consistently demonstrating your dedication to our clients. Methodologies, strategies, and projects are only as good as the individuals who are responsible for implementing them. Your ability to deliver exceptional solutions with clients is unmatched. You are brilliant, humble, willing to do anything for the client's success, and just plain fun to be around. Without hesitation, we will say you are the most talented team of professionals we have ever seen assembled. Thank you for your endless passion.

To Our Families:

For supporting and believing in us all of these years. You have given us perspective, inspiration, and motivation to accomplish great things. We have heard it said that behind every great person there is an exceptional spouse or significant other. We know this to be true. Our lives would not be same without you. Thank you for helping make these dreams a reality.

We are most sincerely grateful to have all of you in our lives.

CONTENTS

THE
FABLE

THE
FIASCO

R andall Phillips was now in the middle of a media nightmare.

It was just minutes after he strode confidently from the network's Green Room onto the set of a popular business news channel's morning show. His makeup in place and the jacket of his suit carefully buttoned, the CEO of CableCorp purposely left behind his talking notes; he would need to speak confidently and freely to assure the millions of viewers that he knew exactly what he was talking about. Randall was not a novice to news conferences. In fact, they were the norm during his career as an executive, but this was his first time in front of the cameras as the leader of the cable company, and he was eager to make a solid first impression.

He had been briefed that the business news channel had run a story the day before on how Netflix was changing the industry as their subscriber base grows and they look for other media assets to acquire. He knew there'd be questions, but CableCorp's communications department had crafted some carefully worded responses for him. He was ready.

With the familiar television lights glaring, the host began the introduction with some friendly banter about Mets baseball. The small talk lasted a few more seconds before the host moved to the first question. However, instead of hitting the Netflix issue, he surprised Randall with a different topic.

"You came to CableCorp almost a year ago with a charge to set things right. The company was hemorrhaging customers, and the complexity of the packages chosen as the company's core offering made service delivery a bit of a debacle. I know your mission was to turn all that around, but based on the recent quarterly filing, I'd jump to the conclusion that this task hasn't been as easy as planned. Now your customers are adding some color to the situation."

Before Randall could open his mouth to respond, the host continued, "I'm sure you've seen it, but this new YouTube video posted by one of your customers isn't exactly what the company needs right now, is it? Do you mind if we take a look?"

Even though this wasn't the Netflix or operating results kind of question that Randall was expecting, he wasn't worried. He had seen the video before and he considered it the work of a vocal minority among his customer base. He and his team had reasoned that it seems no matter what you do, there are always those who feel a need to complain.

This particular video had been out for a couple of weeks and had had a few thousand hits. "This is an open letter to CableCorp," the video began. The mom on the screen looked frazzled; with the camera focused on her face, you could see her frustration. She was often hard to hear because three kids in the background kept fighting, yelling, and running back and forth.

What she managed to convey, though, didn't make CableCorp look good. Her story went something like this. She had promised her daughter that she could watch a DVR copy of her favorite show on Saturday morning if she just finished her milk. She tried to start the show, and when the DVR didn't work, she called customer service. The video mom described in detail all the prompts, selections, wait times, and departments she had been handed off to throughout her call and three subsequent calls before she could get help. All this took place while her young daughter waited to watch her favorite show.

Next came a snide remark regarding CableCorp's on-hold message. "Oh, of course my call is very valuable to you," she muttered. "That's why you keep me waiting without answering like I've got nothing better to do. Do you really have increased call volume or does your call center work as lousy as your cable boxes do?"

To the folks at CableCorp, these complaints had sounded plausible. Their customer service systems and processes had evolved over time to be as cost efficient for the company as possible; sometimes that meant minor inconvenience to customers. But surely this video was just a set of exaggerations by an unhappy, YouTube using customer.

Unfortunately, the poor mom's saga continued. The customer service representative she finally spoke with told her the DVR box was likely damaged and instructed her to disconnect it and return it to the nearest retail service location. She did that. Then the retail service folks told her a technician would have to come to her house to check out the box, and if it couldn't be repaired, they would replace it on the spot.

Next came the video mom's account of the challenges of getting three kids in the car, keeping them in check while waiting at the service location *(for an hour, she said — another likely exaggeration)*, and then heading back home with no resolution.

Once home, she had to call customer service again to schedule the technician's visit. It would be two days — a time period the mom said was exhausting without the chance to grab a few minutes of rest while the kids enjoyed a favorite show.

The video finally reported that a technician showed up. The box was indeed broken, but he didn't have a replacement, so he would have to come back the next day to fix it.

She ended with the declaration that became the title of the video, "My kids hate CableCorp!"

This was the video Randall Phillips was expecting to see when the host directed him to the in-studio monitor. He reflexively glanced at his watch. *The running time would take about eight minutes, far too long for the YouTube crowd,* he thought. *That's probably why it had so few views*

– that and the dull and annoying subject matter.

But as soon as the video started, those in the studio saw a clear sign of surprise flash across his face.

The video didn't open with shaky images of a woman settling into a chair to start her diatribe, as he expected. Instead, the screen showed her face cut and pasted onto a cartoon body with other cartoon people in the scene with her. Someone had taken the sounds from the original video and crafted it into a soundtrack of a rap-style rhythm with short rapidly repeating background sounds of a daughter crying and kids yelling to create a tune. The part of the video where the mom was interrupted by her chair getting whacked with a Wiffle ball bat was also repeated, the sound of the thwack becoming the song's staccato beat.

The cartoon figures played out the story on the screen as the rapid repetition turned the mother's monologue into a rap, the chorus of which was, "my kids hate CableCorp." With the repetition of that phrase throughout the song, it was likely repeated around a hundred times.

As the video closed, the host turned to Randall Phillips with a bit of a smirk and said, "You have to admit, this remix thing is pretty funny– how about those little cartoon guys? The song is catchy too."

Randall Phillips scrambled to organize a response.

The first video was one thing, but this musical remix was offensive. His company was the butt of a joke. "Well, the original video of that poor woman, one of our ten million valued customers," he explained, "was unfortunate. But we felt it was an isolated incident and one we have worked to ensure doesn't happen again."

He continued, "You know, ours is sometimes a complex business and requires the right kind of orchestration to service these issues correctly. They aren't all cookie-cutter problems so it's natural that in rare cases like this, there are mix-ups."

The host jumped in, "Yeah, but you have to admit, that rap was pretty funny."

"It was clever, yes. Perhaps we should get whoever made that video to film our commercials," Randall returned, with a forced smile.

"But back to your initial observation about our turn-around and current churn rates," he said, moving the discussion toward safer ground. "We feel that new products we have recently brought to market have us poised well to meet the needs of our customers. I'm referring to improved on-demand services, premier in-home equipment options, and continued improvements like the addition of mobile service to our convergence of video, voice, and data. We feel we are bringing the right products to the market, and these things will resound with our customer base."

He ended with a smile that suggested he had effectively taken control of the conversation.

"You stated that a situation like the one described in the video is an isolated incident. But how rare are incidents like that?" the host persisted. "Because in the two days that the 'My Kids Hate CableCorp Remix' video has been out, it's received a fair amount of traffic. And the people commenting online about the video all seem to be other customers who corroborate the story. I would tend to think that, in addition to your product and service offering, how you serve your existing customers would likely play at least an equal role in getting your churn rates under control."

"Very true – and like I said, it's something we're looking into and working on now," Randall answered.

The interview continued as the host showed CableCorp's recent stock price performance – a graph that trended lower over the last 12 months. There was a little more small talk and then they went to commercial and Randall got up. The interview was over. T. Boone Pickens was coming on next to talk about natural gas and foreign oil dependence.

As he left the studio and climbed into the waiting car, Randall shook his head. That damn rap video – why didn't anyone tell me that was out there? he muttered to himself. He quickly looked it up on his smartphone. The number of views was already around 175,000. The original video of that mom only had about 5,000 views over two weeks. A few minutes later, he hit refresh on his phone's browser; it was already 200,000 views.

"All it takes is a little mention on TV and this thing takes off like crazy. This stupid customer service thing is going to need a closer look – and fast," he said aloud, even though the only person within earshot was his driver who wasn't likely to respond.

THE
CHALLENGE

D ana Chase had been summoned to the CEO's office before in her three years at CableCorp, but never alone, and never without a thorough heads-up about what to expect. As the company's youngest marketing director, she'd made a name for herself with a website project that received company-wide recognition. The new website improved customer satisfaction and reduced the company's customer service costs as more customers were utilizing the website versus calling into the care centers. As she thought about what this meeting with the CEO could be about, she could only hope that this was a formal recognition of the website effort.

Dana was an implementer. Her boss described her as a great functional leader with drive. However, her team called her "The Queen of 'Git 'er Done" as a play on the popularity of the comedian Larry the Cable Guy, which seemed a fitting honor. It was a bit of a running joke as Dana's team surprised her with a celebration of sorts that featured a poster of Larry the Cable Guy with her face Photoshopped awkwardly in place of his.

Her last project was full of friction and politics, but she still managed to solve a nagging problem for marketing and the company. Though CableCorp had just sunk a sizable investment into freshening the brand, little on the company's website reflected the refocused promise of providing customers more choices. Users had to slog through fairly dull technical language, unimaginative graphics, and even Dana's web savvy husband Sean had trouble finding anything he was looking for on the website.

As it turned out, Dana was excellent at leading large cross functional company initiatives. She was particularly astute at stakeholder management and garnering support of key business leaders. Additionally, Dana understood just enough about CableCorp's technical environment to inspire confidence on the part of the IT department to the point that they felt they had someone working on the business side that understood their efforts and challenges.

The success of the website project gave a huge boost to Dana's personal stock as an accomplished program leader. This newfound reputation led to Dana's consideration to lead other IT-dependent projects that were floundering.

As the elevator pinged and stopped on fifteen, the executive floor, Dana took a deep breath, threw on a confident face, and walked toward Randall Phillips' office. As she reached the office, Randall's assistant smiled. "Mr. Phillips has just finished with his conference call so please go on in."

As Dana entered the office, she announced herself. "Mr. Phillips, I'm here for our meeting." Randall unfolded his 6'4" frame from his leather chair and rose to offer her his hand in greeting. "Dana. Randall Phillips. Thanks for taking time to meet." As if she wouldn't know who he was? As if she'd not be able to work him into her schedule? His smile was engaging enough, but something about his manner didn't feel quite like the demeanor she expected.

That was the end of small talk. "We've got a problem, Dana, and you come highly recommended throughout the company as a problem solver." She smiled at what she assumed was his acknowledgment of the success of the website project, and settled into the seat he offered, being cognizant to not relax too much.

"As you may have heard, we've got a PR nightmare on our hands related to that viral video clip. Worse though, there is truth to the message in the video. If what is depicted in that video happens to be the norm when doing business with CableCorp, we'd better fix it. We've just rebranded the company and made a promise of 'Making Life Easier through Choices.' Obviously, we're failing to deliver on that promise.

"Dana, I've checked with a number of my team members, and your name came up several times, especially after the excellent work you did on the website. But that's just a start in doing better for our customers and getting control of the subscriber churn that's plaguing us."

"I'm not sure if you've seen it but my interview last week has put us in a bad light," he admitted. "But I'm also going to look an equivalent benefit – glass half full if you will – that times like these provide. That video highlighted problems we've had for years, but we've gotten lulled into thinking we should focus elsewhere. I want to see changes in what our customers say about our services, our response to technical calls, and coordination with our call centers, and we need to see them quickly."

So this was behind the invitation to meet with Randall. They'd heard about the quick turnaround on the web issue, and were looking for another quick win. She'd been tapped to deliver. *But relax . . . breathe, she told herself. You've been here before. You can do it again.*

"So how can I help?" Dana asked, careful to keep her voice even and confidently inquisitive.

"We'd like you to lead a project that fixes the major breaks in communications, and improves customer satisfaction responses with our call centers. Cut these wait times and repeat calls. Do what needs to be done so CableCorp gets it right the first time, every time when customers call in. We've already seen what you and your team accomplished with the website and I'm excited to see you do it again with this project. I've asked Nick Barnes from Network Services to serve as project sponsor, but first I wanted to meet with you directly and let you know how important this is to me and the company."

As she rose to shake Randall's hand and exit his office, her mind was already racing with a multitude of unorganized thoughts. Anxiety about her ability to repeat the success of the website project. Excitement about the visibility of the project. Getting a chance to work with Nick Barnes who was a senior vice president. Thinking about who she should recruit for the project. Wondering what to do about those other IT projects she was being considered to run.

Ok, Dana. Just breathe. This isn't your first rodeo, she thought as the elevator door closed.

THE
QUICK FIX

S elections for the project team members began at once. Dana decided to tap one of the IT leads who had been with her through the website project. He had a wealth of knowledge of the company's software applications that were likely contributors of the cross-functional communications issues.

More significantly, she needed excellent subject matter experts from Network Services, Retail Sales, and Customer Care. Given that the resources she would be targeting were always among the most demanded in the company, Dana was hoping to leverage both the CEO's and Nick's sponsorships to actually get them on her team.

Dana was glad to have a reason to begin working more closely with Nick Barnes. She'd been in meetings with him, but they'd never worked together, and she was eager to learn from his experience.

She knew from his bio that he started out as a lineman for a wire line telecommunications company, and worked his way up through the ranks to director through a healthy combination of people smarts and intelligent ideas. The jump to VP came when he moved to an operations position at CableCorp, and six months ago, he was promoted in the senior level reorganization that followed quickly in the wake of Randall Phillips' appointment. Nick went back to Network Services, but this time as Senior Vice President.

The years of front-line experience made him a trusted leader for the field technicians because he knew how to talk their language. More often than not, he hosted his all-hands meetings from one of the technical support centers or the Network Operations Center. And he'd wrangled several members of the senior team into going on ride-alongs with installation technicians to "get a feel for the field," as he told his peers.

He was respected at the senior management table, too, for his no nonsense approach, propensity to speak his mind, solid business sense and ability to help move stalled conversations to a decision. He'd be good for Dana to know, she sensed, and probably had leadership skills that she could learn from.

Dana soon found other reasons to respect him, particularly when she saw how quickly he helped make things happen in the team selection process. After his review of potential team members and a little discussion on why she thought each person was needed, he jumped right in with support. It only took him a couple of phone calls to reluctant bosses to gain people's time. Before she knew it, she felt great about her new team.

"Interesting to see how much easier it is to access the go-to people when the word is out that there is significant executive sponsorship of a project," Nick said to Dana as they reviewed the final team roster.

*   *   *

The team came together and they began planning a week later. As they investigated the problems driving their goal, they settled on three top priorities; two focused on the call centers, and one on field communications.

The call center leads were quick to provide an opinion. Their representatives' knowledge was inadequate, so they were left to give either wrong or misdirected answers to customers. The other glaring problem pointed towards inadequate staffing and performance metrics that created contradictory behaviors. Often, representatives were coached to stop the small talk in order to finish calls that had lasted longer than an acceptable time limit in order to keep their average handle time down. This led to representatives rushing off calls prior to fully resolving customer concerns because they knew their monthly performance rating and subsequent bonus would depend on an acceptable average handle time. The combination of the lack of knowledge and the pressure to wrap up calls on time was not a good one.

These call center issues were not new and the call center leads' recommendations to the team came quickly: develop and deliver better training to the representatives, fix the call center staff forecasting model to add additional representatives during peak call times, and stop focusing on average handle time as a performance metric and instead focus on first call resolution. Surely with the right training, and a little talk time breathing room, the call centers could focus on solving customers' problems instead of passing them off.

The communications challenge was stickier. As the

number of functions involved increased, so did the complexity of the problems. But Dana's push for the right people in the room proved its worth. Their solutions helped to clarify roles and responsibilities among the technicians, call centers, and retail centers. This would aid significantly in understanding when it was best to transfer customers to another function.

A sub-team of call center and retail leads proposed a new way to deliver more timely procedural updates to keep their teams apprised of who was responsible for which customer issues. It wasn't perfect, but at least the right hand would know what the left hand was doing.

Now all that remained was designing a pilot program and measuring results. The team was eager to put their new ideas in place and confident the pilot would show quick results. If all worked as expected, a larger scale company-wide implementation beyond the pilot would be appropriate.

Dana's only significant frustration occurred when the team tried to determine the cause of the service issues. Dana wanted to focus the scope of their discussions and solutions to the issues previously identified by the team, but a few team members seemed insistent on introducing seemingly unrelated topics. Some of the call analytics results pointed to problems with the set-top boxes. Maybe they weren't rare, but happened all the time. Dana wondered if this pointed to quality issues with the hardware they provided.

And the part of the video mom's story where the technician arrived without a new set-top box in his truck was sounding more and more common. As the layers of this issue were peeled back, it was discovered that there was no supply chain connection between Network Services and Retail Sales, leaving each blind to the other's inventory situation. The existing inventory application had been patched together too many times to count as new products and services were introduced in the last few years. Worse, due to cost containment measures, the push to move to a more advanced dispatch system never received funding. Now only the most experienced dispatchers knew their way around all the fixes, shortcuts, and workarounds.

There wasn't any solid data, but the general consensus on her team was that technician staffing wasn't distributed correctly against customer locations. Another issue thought to be impacting customers was training, or the lack thereof. Service installers bragged that they learned more by trial and error or informally from their peers than they ever did from training. In other words, the best training was being delivered by word of mouth from technician-to-technician phone calls – a "solution" that meant more than one technician was often working a problem at the same time.

If these things were true, and the issues real, then her team members were pointing to problems in CableCorp's service delivery that could have provided the fodder for hours of YouTube viewing entertainment.

*   *   *

Toward the end of the pilot planning, her husband Sean had arranged a relaxing dinner at Dana's favorite seafood place. But they'd barely handed their menus back to the waiter before Dana's frustration spilled out.

"When we worked on defining the problem, it was as though we opened Pandora's box," Dana grumbled to Sean, as they waited for their salads to arrive. "All of a sudden, everyone had something to say. I thought we were just getting off track – usually reining them back in works pretty well.

"But this is different. They were kind of intense, like someone had finally asked them to point out the real problems in our business, and they weren't going to stop until got everything off their chest. To their credit, these weren't just nit-picky issues. They were describing some pretty big stuff, things that need to be corrected or they'll cost us more customers."

Sean knew when his wife got like this that his best approach was to let her work it through at her own pace, so they sat quietly for a moment. But the break in their conversation only served to allow them to overhear the discussion at the next table. "Hey!" Sean hissed. "Listen. That guy is talking about the YouTube video."

They tuned in to the conversation and listened, as a man with his back to Dana vigorously recounted the video storyline in gory detail to his companions: a red-haired woman sitting next to him and, across from them, a striking blonde with a shorter, balding man. He covered it all: the call center mess up, the snappy rap tune, the idiot technician, and the retail store run-around, right down to the squalling kids.

Dana cringed and slid down a little in her chair. Hopefully this conversation would die soon. But it didn't. "I could make my own video about my billing issues with CableCorp," the blonde woman across from him jumped in.

"Last year I signed up with CableCorp to get the $29 a month new subscriber deal based on what the sales rep told me. But six months later my bill jumped to $89 a month. Now they tell me the original rep I talked with had it wrong . . . nothing they can do."

The red-haired woman was quick to agree. "I'd like to tell them what they can do with their slogan about making life easier. I grind my teeth every time I see those ads on TV!"

The waiter's arrival with their orders interrupted the conversation. "Who needed customer surveys and comment cards with feedback like this dumped right in my lap?" she said quietly to Sean as she turned to her salad. She'd heard unresolved issues from her team, but these irate customers brought them into focus even more forcefully.

Now she was stuck with a new level of questions. Were they just filling a hole in the dam with putty while a tidal wave built up behind it? She pulled out her phone and sent a text to Nick. "Nick, would love to talk tomorrow a.m. if possible. I need your advice."

* * *

Nick moved an early morning appointment to make time for her before the team convened for the day. After a night of thinking things through, Dana was calmer now, and the issues were clearer.

"I'm wondering if we are prescribing aspirin to treat an aneurysm," she confessed. "It was one thing to hear my team surface inconsistencies in the way we deliver on our brand promises. But hearing customers commiserating with their friends that we aren't who we say we are and we don't do what we say we will – well, that makes it even more real.

"Nick, I'm wondering now if we're doing the company a disservice by providing only a small solution to a whole series of problems that are actually linked together. The practical side of me says we'd be better off solving some of these smaller issues. I can't imagine how we'd begin to address everything – it would mean dozens of projects like this one, maybe more. But then I think about the fact that even if we solved all these issues, we are only reacting to our current problems. We need to think more strategically."

"You can stop me anytime here," she grinned, catching herself.

"I'm not stopping you because I'm busy listening, Dana," Nick said. "I've seen exactly what you are discovering. If you look at the company from our customers' point of view, we interact with them in a whole lot of ways as they investigate us, decide to buy from us, and then use our services. You and the team are pointing out inconsistencies in how we deliver on all those opportunities. And it's those inconsistencies that can cost us customers.

"Unfortunately, we're a pretty tactical company, kind of like my kid's 'whack-a-mole' game. You know the one; you push one mole down just to have another pop up in a different place. That's us, only with these issues instead. We take care of brand alignment on the web, or a few call center issues, and they get attention because they're causing us the biggest pain. But before we get to solve the real problems, another big pain hits us, and we've moved on to something else. Over time, all we have done is apply a bunch of band-aids to a dying patient. It will take a systemic overhaul in how we support customers to make a difference, but I don't think we have the appetite for it."

Nick paused. "Did anyone warn you about these rants of mine?" he asked Dana.

"I like ranting," Dana assured him. "It means we're out of the polite small talk phase and getting into the stuff that matters."

"Well, that's all the ranting I have planned for today," Nick said. "I'd suggest you store these observations away. Certainly don't abandon them, but now isn't the time to push for action. When you've been tasked by Randall to solve an issue and you need quick turnaround and fast results, political prudence says you focus there and nowhere else. Make sense?"

It did, of course, so Dana headed for the planning room. The project team was waiting and they had a pilot to design.

*   *   *

In the weeks ahead, the pilot went off with only minor glitches, much to Dana's relief. Better still, the interventions they'd designed were proving out. Customer satisfaction scores increased for customers touched by the pilot, making a solid case for company-wide implementation.

News of the pilot's success spread quickly, fueled by a splashy story on the company's internal website about the team's success. The article came with a prominently displayed photo of Dana with arms crossed leaning against an outside wall of the headquarters building donning a serious look on her face. Although it appeared that Dana was the sole reason for success, she knew better, and shifted attention to the team with her quotes throughout the article.

All this notoriety would surely set the stage for an easy approval of the larger implementation, Dana told herself. As the attention grew, she noticed that her nagging concerns about the bigger, broader issues that were so eloquently highlighted by the customers she and Sean overheard during her dinner grew fainter. She reasoned with herself that a company could only do so much at a time.

Faint as it was, she still had a sense that perhaps in leading the project she was winning a battle, but helping falsely prop the company up to lose the bigger war for customers. However, she brushed her suspicions aside, realizing her busy week ahead needed her focus now. She was scheduled to attend a customer experience conference, and would also need to gather her thoughts on preparing the executive presentation regarding the pilot's results. The presentation would cover the team's approach to the pilot and its results, and would end with an approval request for the budget and timeline to roll everything out across the company.

No time to entertain doubts now.

THE
DISCOVERY

The conference in Atlanta would be an excellent opportunity for Dana to listen and learn about what other companies and thought leaders were doing in the realm of customer experience. The whole conference was focused on the topic and seemed to fit with the events of the last couple weeks perfectly.

As a bonus, Dana's advisor and friend, Jane Friedman, was scheduled to speak. With Jane's busy teaching schedule and an active consulting practice, getting a piece of her time was a challenge. However, a couple of days in a new city and a more flexible schedule might allow for some of the mentoring Jane always seemed willing to provide.

As she checked into the Hyatt in downtown Atlanta Tuesday afternoon, Dana could feel her energy rising. Maybe it was the pleasure of being able to think about something other than the immediate issues at CableCorp. Nick had reviewed her presentation to the senior team and they both felt she was ready. The remaining hurdle for the post-pilot implementation was funding, as a company wide effort would require a $20 million investment. In spite of the size, Nick was confident that the approval would come given the project's visibility and CableCorp's imperative to act quickly.

A voice from across the hotel lobby pulled her out of her thoughts and back to the conference. "Dana! Did you bring your running shoes?"

Jane Friedman waved her greeting, and Dana hurried to meet her. "You bet! The concierge is mapping out a route as we speak. Are you still game?"

Jane laughed. "I have a half-marathon to get ready for and I'm not exactly in half-marathon shape, so you can count me in."

"Well, I'll try to take it easy on you since I need you to actually have breath to talk. I do hope you still like to talk while you run," Dana said, "because we have some serious catching up to do. You'll be amused to hear I'm now running a project that has me hanging out with folks like Larry the Cable guy and worrying about average handle times in call centers. 'Dana Chase, The Marketer' – or perhaps the former marketer – has taken on a new persona."

"Then we do have a lot to catch up on," Jane agreed. "You might have seen in the brochure that I'm leading a session here, so I'm meeting with my co-presenter tonight. But it's only 4:00 now. We've got time to go for a good run before my dinner with him. And how about dinner together tomorrow night? I know a great Italian place near here. We'll practice carb loading. As you can tell I'm in better shape for that."

Plans set, Dana left to settle in. Jane would love the YouTube story that generated her current project. It might just give her material for one of the anecdotes that made her marketing classes the most enjoyable of Dana's college courses.

During the next day's conference sessions, Dana heard ideas that pushed her to think differently about CableCorp's marketing efforts.

For instance, one speaker challenged them to ask, "In which ways do you want your customers to react to you? Do you want to empower them, give them value, wow them, simplify their lives, or make them cool?" Would

CableCorp describe itself as having a "simplify their lives" message, or did it want to be more? She liked the straightforwardness of the five options, and the positive energy they evoked.

As the day progressed, her initial burst of enthusiasm was replaced by thoughtfulness. This customer experience stuff wasn't what she'd assumed initially. The sessions focused consistently on customer loyalty and advocacy, not just satisfaction, and on the gains that can come when your customers become true believers in the brand.

Wednesday night at dinner, Jane listened as Dana fed back her ah-ha moments from the sessions. "But here's the problem," Dana concluded. "I see the feel-good sense of wanting to delight every customer every time every way. But get real. We both know the customer isn't always right. Sometimes they can be unreasonable and want you to give your service away for free. Surely we'd go broke if we tried an approach like this."

With a slight grin, Jane asked Dana, "Are you interested in dessert?" Dana knew by the look on her face that she had something to add to the conversation and she was eager to hear it.

"Of course I want dessert. If I'm going to eat a 1500 calorie Italian pasta dish, I might as well go all the way!"

Dana said with a smile. "I know you have an opinion about this, so what are thinking?"

"Your point is well-taken, Dana," Jane smiled. "That delight-every-time" premise drove some of the early customer experience work, but it has moved beyond it now. The new thinking, and what I believe in, is that a great customer experience has to support the company's mission and align with its brand promise. So when the idea of great customer experience is confused with great customer service, I have to caution people that they are only looking at one small slice of the overall picture. Great customer service best aids the customer experience if the company's brand promise says they provide great customer service. And you know enough about brand work to know that no one tries to be all things to all buyers, at least not the most successful companies."

Dana nodded as she poured cream into her coffee. "We've just finished some work on brand realignment, and for us it's about making life easier by increasing customers' choices. We don't promise the lowest prices or the hottest, edgiest on-demand content. It's what you taught in the classroom, Jane, about delivering against the expectations you set."

Jane looked pleased to hear her former student recalling class content like this. "You must have gotten an A the day we talked about the differing service expectations of Nordstrom's and Wal-Mart's customers. Remember the survey that was provided to customers regarding their experiences? If you can recall, we asked a group of customers to tell us about great service and poor service.

We had Wal-Mart come up quite frequently in the poor service area; things like the aisles being in disarray, warehouse feel, tacky décor, unfriendly cashiers. But then we asked whether they would return to Wal-Mart to purchase again. Nearly 98% said they would because they were more interested in getting the lowest price than in most other things. So Wal-Mart's customer experience is largely dependent upon its ability to deliver on the promise of low prices, much more so than having friendly cashiers.

"Point is, of course, that your brand promise and profitability strategy shape decisions about what makes a great experience for your customers," Jane confirmed. "But what's new about the 'experience' part of what you're hearing is this: your delivery can't be hit or miss. In order to win the long-term loyalty you heard talked about so much about today, companies have to get it right every time a customer interacts with them throughout the duration of their relationship.

"That means the experience is bigger than the product or service they are paying for. It's in what they see on billboards, what they hear on TV, what they experience in the stores, how they feel after a call with a rep. Customers are influenced by what they find on the website, what their friends and friend's friends are saying on Facebook, whether they can understand their monthly bill, and what patronizing the company says about them as a person. And let me get on my soapbox for a moment around advertising. I cannot emphasize enough how important it is to make sure your advertising team is fully aligned with customer experience and brand strategy messages. If I had a nickel for each time I witnessed an outside advertising company create a commercial that was more geared toward winning a creative award from the ad industry than expressing the brand promises of their clients, I'd be retired now.

"Let me give you a real example," Jane continued. "I did some consulting work a few years ago for a large home improvement store whose brand promise was to 'Help You Get It Done.' They had huge stores with every piece of hardware that you could imagine; my husband absolutely loves the place," Jane paused. "But when the company began to lose market share – they couldn't figure out why. That was, until I dug in a little deeper with some of their customers," she explained.

Dana listened carefully. "What I found," Jane explained, "was that they clearly weren't delivering on their brand promise. Most of the customers had a clear expectation that the company would deliver on their brand promise to 'Help Them Get It Done.' What they found online and in the stores, however, was far from helpful.

"Apparently, customers would go to the store with a specific project or issue – and then couldn't find an associate to help them. And when they did – they didn't get the answers they needed, or worse yet, they received bad advice." Jane continued, "The customers I spoke with were extremely vocal, stating that they would never shop there again. The company had made a brand promise, but when the customer experience didn't live up to the promise, customers began leaving in droves."

Dana asked, "What did they do to fix it?"

"Well, there was no quick fix. They had to completely revamp the end-to-end customer experience to ensure alignment with their brand promise. For example, the website was updated with self help tips, and they rolled out an entirely new customer service model." Jane continued, "It wasn't about fixing a single point of interaction or customer service issue; all aspects of the customer experience had to be aligned with their brand promise. It eventually paid off in a big way; they're now growing faster than ever," she concluded.

They were quiet in the cab back to the hotel as Dana processed their conversation. It was now easier to see some things CableCorp was missing. They had not clarified to groups outside of marketing what the brand promise meant. Therefore, in operational decisions and projects, the question of how those decisions should be influenced by the brand promise wasn't even considered.

She also doubted that anyone had looked at work through the lens of an end-to-end customer relationship. Indeed, their one-off, pain-instigated prioritization of solutions drove an opposite way of thinking. They were always too busy with point solutions targeted at the squeakiest wheel to focus on the big picture and moving in ways that drove the most value for both the customer and the company.

Dana was eager to discuss her new revelation with Nick. She left him another voicemail with a few things she'd learned from her talk with Jane, and promised a call on Thursday.

Nick had already responded by the time Dana checked her smartphone before the next morning's session. *How early does this guy get started anyway?* she wondered to herself as she read his message.

One thing was clear: She'd created intrigue with her voice message. "Looks like some of what you're learning confirms we were on target in our observations about the need for strategic thinking to drive a better customer experience," he wrote. "And you're also coming up with more convincing arguments than what we generated. How about the cost/benefit of all this?"

Her response was quick. "Got it covered," she wrote back. "10:30 session on business cases led by my MBA advisor. She knows her stuff. I will check in after."

Indeed, Jane's presentation on the business viability of customer experience didn't disappoint. She'd compiled metrics from several companies that had completed customer experience transformations and the trends were clear. One report showed, for example, that just a modest improvement in customer experience had driven an increase in incremental revenue of between $250 and $300 million for every $1 billion in annual sales.

Dana decided she'd ask Jane for the presentation in order to forward to Nick. CableCorp executives generally tuned out when it came to soft stuff, but they paid attention to anything that hit the bottom line.

The co-presenter was an executive from a property-casualty insurance company Jane had helped through what they called their "customer experience strategy implementation." The process took eighteen months and was not without glitches, especially when it came to motivating the functional leads to release enough control so more strategic changes could be put in place. But the company's financial outcomes matched Jane's earlier data, and their roadmap and lessons learned only made the process seem more do-able in Dana's mind.

Dana flew home Thursday night with her head buzzing with thoughts. Now the project she had been so jazzed about presenting on Monday seemed almost counterproductive. She was confident they'd fix some of the call center and communications glitches and this would certainly have a positive impact on the customer experience and the company, but these changes would not address all of the larger issues presented by her team.

When they met Friday for a final check-in, Nick made it clear he'd been impressed with the numbers he'd seen. "Last week at this time we both had some educated guesses, or rants on my part, about what the company should be doing differently regarding customer experience," he reflected to Dana. "But what you've shown this week convinces me that CableCorp will not be able to achieve its longer term vision and shareholder returns if we don't address the larger strategic issues."

Dana waited. "So, are you convinced enough we ought to change the proposal?" she asked.

He shook his head. "I'm intrigued and excited," he said, "but not crazy! The team's completed a lot of excellent work and the project will provide benefits. I think we should move forward with the proposal as is, and then you and I can work on a new one to address the more holistic picture. When we knock it out of the park on this project, we should gain momentum for more effort in this space."

THE
RIGHT-ANGLE
TURN

When Dana saw that she was the first to arrive in the boardroom Monday morning, she wondered if she'd be perceived as prompt or perhaps just eager.

Both were probably true, she told herself, especially today. As others filed in, she mentally rehearsed the coaching Nick had provided about what to expect from the other members of the executive committee.

"You know Alex from Marketing pretty well, of course, so there'll be no surprises there. And both the Consumer and Business Market presidents are obviously sales guys – amiable and reasonable. They'll both profit from the results of the project, so I doubt they'll ask many questions. Most of the others vary. They do a lot of listening and weigh in when asked, but generally aren't that outspoken.

"But you'll enjoy seeing Randall Phillips in action," Nick continued. "He's a quick decision maker in a way that almost seems off the cuff. But he's smart enough that nothing with him is really off the cuff. When he decides, it's a done deal."

Nick did caution her, however, about the CFO. "It is unfortunate Stuart Betts couldn't attend when we approved the original pilot project," he told her. "Of course maybe it's not so unfortunate, because the project may never have gotten off the ground if he'd been weighing in for the pilot. You've probably heard most of us affectionately call him 'Dr. No.' Don't get me wrong, Stuart is a great guy. And as the CFO, his primary responsibility is to make sure that we are making sound financial decisions, but this sometimes puts him in the role of 'bad cop' during these project approvals."

Dana knew Stuart's reputation well, and affection never went along with the descriptors of him. She knew, too, he was as bright as he was unrelentingly committed to guaranteeing good news for the quarterly earnings reports. She expected tough questions from Stuart, even if this work began at the CEO's request.

Nick agreed. "Stuart is afraid of no one. And Randall is working hard to soften his often-harsh edge. But you can expect that this is still a work in progress, so don't let it make you sweat," Nick said with a reassuring smile.

The senior team had now assembled and Stuart's choice to position himself directly across from Dana didn't add to her comfort level. But as her turn came on the agenda and she began the presentation, she was careful not to avoid him, making sure her expression stayed strong and confident.

She was barely into the third slide before he leaned back and folded his arms across his chest. This was definitely not a posture of support, even though both the Consumer and Business leads seemed to be giving encouraging nods. *You expected an edge, he hasn't objected yet,* she reminded herself as she went on to describe the outcome of the pilot.

"What questions do you have?" she asked.

Stuart was first to respond, now leaning toward her with what Dana interpreted as a look of distrust. Or suspicion, maybe? Either way, it wasn't a comfortable look.

"The recommendations you've made," he started. "Tell me more."

She paused. A simple enough request, except his version of asking about the recommendations sounded a whole lot more like an inquisition about the cost justifications.

Before she could answer, he said, "These changes – increased staffing and training for the call centers? We're not just talking about expenses for more reps and the expense of developing the training, but lost time when the reps are off the phones being trained. And there are reasons why we haven't given the reps power to distribute credits in the past...these spend decisions are being made by people with no accountability for profits or losses."

She drew a breath to answer, but he decided to hold the floor.

"Look. All of you know our financials were off last quarter, and nothing in this proposal looks like it will help us next quarter. In fact, just the opposite; it may hurt us with higher costs against declining revenue.

"Wasn't it less than two years ago that we dumped money into a process re-engineering program and the Voice of the Customer application that were supposed to address some of these customer issues? We need to wait for those initiatives to pay off before allocating more money to this problem. Otherwise, we might find ourselves guilty of throwing good money after bad!"

Dana had never seen the air drain out of a room so quickly, or so completely. She knew Stuart would be tough, but this was the first time to see it, and feel it, for herself. *Where was Randall Phillips? The CEO trumps everyone, doesn't he? After all, he did ask me to run with this effort, right?* Dana glanced at his end of the table. He sat quietly, leaning back, tapping the table with a pen, seemingly waiting for other responses. Was all their work about to be tanked without anyone's protest?

Nick cleared his throat. "You all know I'm the sponsor of this project," he began. All right, Dana thought. *This is what a sponsor is for – to support and advocate in these meetings when necessary.*

"I'm project sponsor," he repeated, "but...but I have to say, I agree with Stuart."

Dana couldn't believe what she was hearing.

"I agree," Nick repeated, "I almost feel irresponsible in making this claim here now...as I worked with Dana and the team to develop this recommendation to move forward, but Stuart's points are well taken. Some of the projects we've approved in the past few years failed to provide the value they promised. And I hate to admit this because a couple of these took place in my shop."

His vulnerability caught others off guard. But his openness must have emboldened the Consumer Markets president. "Consumer sponsored one of them, too, actually," he admitted. "I think the problem is that we get pretty reactionary around here instead of keeping our view at a strategic level."

A couple of others nodded their agreement, and there was a moment of silence.

Nick spoke again. "Look, I said I agree with the financials. But I have recently realized something else. I've been guilty of looking at some things backwards, and I don't think I'm the only one here doing it. I have supported some of these projects because it appeared they'd be a good short term fix for a pressing problem area that was causing issues and most importantly, customer loss.

"I know we all care about CableCorp's success, but frankly I'm tired of watching us put on blinders and ignore our bigger issues. It's killing our reputation and hurting our bottom line. If we continue down this path, our competition will tear us apart." He went on, "If we really want to grow revenues at this company, profitable revenues, then we need to think differently. Instead of another band aid, I'd suggest that we'd be better off investing our money in a more strategic approach to transforming our customer experience, an approach that involves all functions and helps us to deliver on the promise of our brand."

Nobody said anything.

"I've seen a number of proven case studies where customers were actually willing to pay *more* for a superior experience – case studies that focused on and drove top-line revenue growth while making a huge dent in churn. Maybe our approach shouldn't be to spend less, but rather to spend differently on a broader program with a longer term view consistent with our company's vision of making life easier for our customers."

Now it was Stuart's turn. He took off his glasses and looked at Nick. "Since you're talking about revenue increases, you've got my attention," he said. "It's these continual increases in expenditures without the subsequent bottom line return that I get so tired of hearing about, so this might be interesting if there's more and it makes sense."

This small opening was enough for Nick, and he recounted the highlights of the business cases he and Dana had reviewed. First the insurance company example – their size and value were close to CableCorp's, and their turnaround in profitability was recent. He then moved to other examples and, in each case, he highlighted the correlation between increases in customer experience and company profitability. It was the right lead message, as the entire room was engaged as he spoke.

"Can you imagine what it would be like if we didn't react to every small change in the marketplace? If we stood firm knowing that our brand promises resonated with our customers and it resulted in greater market share? That we were deliberate in our actions and caused other companies to take notice? I can. And I don't think we will thrive and achieve our subscriber or revenue forecast without it. I think this is imperative for us."

"So here's my proposal. We direct the design of a new   customer experience, this time using a strategic approach that looks at all the ways we interact with a customer. We then figure out the best ways to make these reflect our brand. It would be low cost and low risk, but we would produce recommendations with a better chance of delivering results."

Now Randall sat up straighter. "Keeping expenses in line – that's important, Stuart," he said, looking directly at the CFO. "But it is investments – the right investments, strategic investments – that will get us to a profitable future."

"I'm not sure how long it would take to build the strategy you mentioned but committing resources for three months seems reasonable to me," the CEO said with an edge of finality in his voice. "I'm thinking that a first-class, cross-functional team could be tasked to get started and come back with recommendations on how to proceed."

"Nick," he paused, "why don't you sponsor this with Dana's help? You helped bring this need into focus for us so I think it makes sense that you are involved."

The decisiveness in the CEO's tone had clearly shifted the direction in the room. Now with a $20 million program no longer in play, the CFO could offer little resistance.

"Let's go with this," Randall said, closing the discussion, and he turned to Dana. "It looks like you have a new job."

THE
RESTART

"If you act enthusiastic, you'll be enthusiastic and enthusiasm is contagious!" Dana could hear her dad's admonition as clearly as if he was walking beside her as she headed for Nick's office.

This morning she needed the reminder because she was feeling more anxious than enthusiastic. Her last project, the *YouTube Retake* as it had come to be known around the company, had definitely been exciting. The new challenge that Dana now faced should have increased that excitement by a factor of ten. Instead, the daunting task of aligning leaders from across the company was displacing any excitement with fear and doubt.

She wanted larger responsibility; this project could hold the key to a whole new relationship with customers, one that could drive loyalty and profits for years to come. And she wanted visibility; but Dana hadn't imagined her big break coming like this. Yes, Randall had approved a three-month effort to create a new customer experience strategy, mostly due to his confidence in Nick's down-to-earth good sense. But even her sponsor heard the challenge to "prove it" in Randall's voice.

Dana found herself more and more invested in the project and loyal to Nick. He'd stuck out his neck when he championed a long shot and came away with a restart, mostly on the basis of his reputation. *If he has to take a hit for someone, I don't want it to be me, Dana told herself resolutely. We have to make this happen.*

From the reviews provided by others, the cross functional team she'd been able to assemble brought exceptional talent along with some interesting personalities. It would have been easiest to start with the team she'd just led for the customer service pilot, but the strategic focus and scope of this new assignment required some different players. She hadn't worked with any of them, except for one. Unfortunately, she knew she could expect plenty of grief from him – so much for friendly familiar faces in the room. *Looks like we'll need to start over to make sure that this team is comfortable enough with each other to share the truth,* she thought as she reviewed the team list.

Arnie Hansen was an up-and-coming sales leader, and if you weren't sure of that, he'd find ways to let you know – especially the "up-and-coming" part. A recent graduate of an esteemed business school, he'd been recruited for an accelerated, rotation-based development program designed to fast-track new leaders.

Somehow, early in his tenure, some of the program participants were invited to golf with the CEO and some of his team. Ever since then, Arnie believed that trading wits with a few of the executives for 18 holes had given him some sort of special privilege not appointed to others in the company. He would often challenge people, claiming to have a direct channel to the executive suite, which more often than not made any challenger back down. Although the now infamous round of golf had long passed, Arnie's own over-confidence kept him oblivious to what many of the executives actually thought of him. Dana actually questioned how long he would be with the company and why Nick would have ever allowed his assignment to this project.

Dana had already heard through the grapevine that

he'd been telling others this project should have belonged to the Sales team. Customers, after all, were rightfully their domain. *Maybe this assignment was a development opportunity for him, Dana reassured herself. Wonder if I'm going to want to find a way to develop him right off the project.* Only time would tell.

Melinda Scott, a Customer Service manager, was her second team member. Dana had met her once during the pilot, and had enjoyed her company and knowledge about Customer Service. Melinda knew the call centers and cared about what she called "her reps." Dana was sure that after ten years of managing in the call center world, Melinda was sure to have heard every question and every complaint numerous times. *Hopefully she'll bring some solutions to the table along with those complaints,* Dana thought.

"I want happy reps," Melinda had told someone, "because happy reps make for happy customers. Put me on that project and I'll give my best."

The last half of the team brought a different set of challenges. Sharon Nelson from Network Services was the one Dana most looked forward to meeting. She was known as a 'big picture' person and full of energy. With any luck, she'd be a strong asset in keeping the team focused strategically. And because her experience and personality were so easy to respect, she'd win a hearing, Dana was sure.

Sharon started years ago in a wire line telecommunications company as a service technician, a job her dad had helped her get. She was a single mom with two young children, and the job paid better than anything else in the town. She made it work, and like Nick, she moved up through the ranks of management. In fact, she'd followed him to CableCorp when he made the move, so it was his request that allowed her to leave the field for this project.

The IT group had provided Dana's biggest unknown from a management perspective. Roger McDaniels had been a key player two years before in the process re-engineering project that ended up costing big bucks, mostly in consulting fees from some big international firm that brought a sizeable team on-site for a number of months. After that hefty investment, it had produced little return for the effort when CableCorp was left with reams of process documentation but little direction on what to do next and how to start. From what Dana had heard, he believed deeply in the process work and carried a chip on his shoulder the size of Texas regarding the fact that the company had pulled the plug on the project.

He took it as a personal affront that money had been okayed for this "customer experience stuff" and had been assigned to the project not because he wanted to be a part of it, but because there was no one else available who knew the applications and systems the way he did.

CableCorp had learned a long time ago they needed to include IT representation when these new projects kicked off, because decisions sometimes were made that affected them but didn't fit their architectural or software standards and philosophies. "Okay," Dana said out loud. She'd been assigned a project team that she barely knew to take on a project in an area that the company had little experience or expertise in. "Good thing I'm addicted to challenges," Dana shook her head, and headed off to Nick's office for their scheduled meeting.

*   *   *

Nick had been generous with his time in helping to plan the approach. "If I were you, I'd choose focus over fancy footwork on this one," Nick had counseled, and Dana agreed. "I'd keep the approach simple – clarify the current state, define the end state, and come up with some rock-solid recommendations to close the gap."

"We are thinking alike on the approach," Dana told him. "When the content is unfamiliar, sticking with a straightforward gap analysis makes sense."

"The key to this work will come from what you learned at the conference. CableCorp's big miss has been in evaluating our customer relationship exclusively from our company's view, rather than starting with the customers' perspective; not only what they want and need from us but also what we have promised to them. I think if you keep customers clearly in your line of sight during each step of the gap analysis, you'll get to where you need to be."

Dana left Nick's office to prepare for the project kick-off that was only days away.

Since marketers are known for market analysis and data, Dana had decided to live up to her function's reputation, and had plastered the planning room with poster-size info-nuggets about CableCorp's customers – who they were, demographics, preferences, as many factoids as she could quickly pull from the marketing databases. She even posted one particular customer's quote that drove the point home:

> *CableCorp hasn't made my life any easier.*
> *I can't seem to get anything to work right –*
> *and they can't seem to help me.*

She had emailed an agenda, case studies, and market research materials to the participants in advance. As usual, Dana was well prepared, but that didn't keep that feeling of anxiety from creeping in as she waited for her new project team to enter the room.

Nick kicked off the meeting with the story of the project's inception, and an explanation of the team's charter. "You've got your work cut out for you," he told them, "because you'll be exploring new ground. We aren't putting together a cross-functional approach like this just to implement some fixes and stick band-aids on our issues. We're looking for you to develop our long-term customer experience strategy. Randall Phillips has told me that this project is his number one priority right now. The strategy that you develop will set our direction for years to come. I hope you share my excitement as we really have not approached our business issues this way in the past and you are truly blazing new trails."

"No pressure," Dana quipped to ease a bit of the pressure in the room.

She jumped in to start the introductions and opened first with some personal information: her work history in hopes of building respect, a struggle or two in hopes she'd gain their trust, and a word about her husband Sean and the "money pit" house they were bent on remodeling. She remembered a quote from years prior that stated,

"Teams will not trust the message unless they trust the messenger." Since hearing this, she had always implemented a get-to-know-her introduction with every team she led. Though certainly not a one-time effort, she hoped it was a good start to developing a positive team dynamic.

After the others had finished with their introductions, she went straight to the work at hand. "Since customer experience begins with 'customer', that's where we're going to begin, as well," she stated, and explained the gap analysis approach they'd be using.

"To determine current state, we're going to document all we know about the customer lifecycle – all the things they actually do in their interactions with us during the entire time they are our customers.

"In order to get us started," Dana said, "I want you to think about the customer lifecycle in three stages that include Attraction, Interaction, and Cultivation. These stages represent the before, during, and after states for our customer. Simply put, we want to know how and why customers come to us, how they interact with us, and why they stick around or, God forbid, leave.

"From your view, what is the first step in our customer experience lifecycle?" Dana started. At first, nobody spoke. The silence lasted long enough that Dana wondered if she needed a different approach. Fortunately, Arnie broke the silence, beginning confidently.

"Ah... the first steps are to make them aware of us. You can't sell to people who don't know you exist. And we've got a bunch of ways to do that – it's what our TV ads are designed for, and why we produce the mailers we do. And our prospecting applications tie to data bases..."

Dana broke in. "Arnie, thank you for being bold with the first response. Your answer is correct in that it is what we do as a company. But for this first activity we need to turn the question around. Pretend you're a customer. How do you start your process of choosing a cable, Internet, and/or telephone provider?"

Roger would have none of it. "How can we legitimately be talking about customers at this point? Aren't they just prospects until they buy something from us? So, isn't this really a 'prospect experience lifecycle' we're dreaming up here? Can't give good answers until we're all clear we're answering the right question, you know."

Dana worked consciously to keep the irritation she felt out of her voice. "Technically correct, Roger," she responded. "But for the sake of this discussion I would like to bend our definitions a little."

Roger came back in a tone edged in sarcasm. "Well,

if we're going to just take a stab at defining the problem we're solving, maybe we can just take a stab at answers, too. How about if we write down all that stuff prospects *try* to experience from us, like that woman in the video? All she wanted was a control box that worked consistently, and an installer who would come without her waiting at home all day to let him in, and getting straight answers when she called us…is that what you're looking for?"

Dana wondered if Roger was aware others in the room actually represented some of the functions he had disparaged, but she decided to let it go. *Was this how the day was going to proceed?* Dana thought while she took a deep breath and replied, "Well, we could start there, Roger, but then we'd only be looking at the fires without really understanding what's causing the fires in the first place."

"I guess I did a poor job in explaining," Dana told the team as she moved to the flip chart and began to write. "A big picture way to look at the question is this: at the highest level, customers go through stages in their interactions with us. We'll label them 'Shop,' 'Buy' and 'Use.'" And she wrote all three on the board.

"But there are many more than those three . . ." Melinda protested.

"I agree," Dana nodded. "Just consider these three as

categories. We're going to list some of those things you are thinking about as customer activities when we expand on each of these categories. Activities related to "Buy" for example, might be things like choosing the service plan or signing the agreement. Does that make sense?"

It must have connected for Melinda, because she jumped in quickly. "Okay, well, they first have to shop for cable service. So they've got to recognize they need –or maybe want – entertainment and data services in their home. That's the start, right? Then like Arnie said, they have to become aware of our brand and our products and services. They might be looking at other providers, too, and comparing them against us. Am I on the right track here?"

Soon the team began to click and the list grew, with Arnie and Melinda contributing more aggressively to ideas about shopping and buying. Dana even added some of her own thoughts from her marketing experience. Sharon joined Melinda to outline how customers use Ca-bleCorp services and get help when they need it.

Before long, Dana had things like "Pay Bill" on the flipchart, under which the team began to expand into identifiable components, like online billing and online bill pay, which then involved logging on to the website. And a mailed bill meant receiving it, writing a check, and then sending it off. The picture of what it meant for a customer to interact with CableCorp was beginning to show more complexity.

Roger opted to not contribute. His open laptop seemed to hold his attention while the others engaged in sharing what they knew. Knowing the importance of obtaining all functional views surrounding this project, Dana asked for Roger's input, but he mumbled something about already charting all these components during his process re-engineering days and not really needing to do it again.

Dana felt the back of her neck redden. Was it against company policy to slap an employee if he really, really deserved it, she wondered? But before she could speak, Sharon challenged him. "That's probably just as well," she said to him dryly. "I've seen the re-engineering stuff. You'd have us lost in the weeds in four minutes."

That was all Roger needed to hear. Motivated by Sharon's clear challenge to his abilities, without a word he shut his laptop and went for a marker. In a flurry of blue ink, the charts for "Buy" and "Use" were soon covered with detail-level process activities. "I hope you have plenty of flip charts," he warned Dana. "I've got plenty more where these came from."

"Okay, okay," Sharon said to him. "You've made your

point. But your suggestions are overkill. We only need about ten of these activities – we've got to stay high-level in our view of customers or we'll never get this gap analysis done."

Now Roger had engaged, but it was clearly to keep the focus on his expertise. "Ten? We need hundreds of workflows to really understand the details of how things really work in this company." Dana let him continue for a couple of minutes before carefully stepping in.

"Roger is right. We will eventually need to understand the details of how things work, and that may happen at a later stage of our effort," Dana explained. "Roger, this is exactly why you are an integral part of this team. Your knowledge about CableCorp's systems is incredibly deep. I want to see if we can step out of our comfort areas and really almost forget our knowledge of CableCorp for a moment and step into the shoes of the customer."

Dana paused, then continued, "What we need to define is the customer experience process – from the customer's perspective – not ours – and since we don't have that defined as a company yet, we have to start at a high level." Then she added, "We've been at this for a long time and there is a lot of great information here. Why don't we call it a day, I can capture what we have for our use later and you guys can spend the remainder of the day catching up on emails or doing whatever is needed."

Dana stayed an hour after the team departed, logging information from the day's discussion and documenting the twelve activities that fell under the "Shop," "Buy" and "Use" categories.

As she collected her laptop and got ready to leave, she called Nick to give him a quick report on their progress. "Nick, it was painful at the beginning. I couldn't get them to think from the customer's perspective. Roger is clearly still bitter about the process re-engineering work being cancelled and I think he wanted to take it out on this effort. That said, we did make some progress and I'll send you the notes from what we have today if you're interested," Dana paused for a response.

"Sounds like you're off to a good start," he encouraged her. "You can send your notes from today, but I'll probably focus more on your final recommendations unless you want me more involved. Just let me know. I expect you're going to move fairly soon to the company's view of all these interactions, the customer touch points, as your conference staff called them. Once the team gets over to more familiar ground, I'll bet your pace of work picks up."

She hoped he was right.

The following morning, Dana led with a quick introduction to customer touch points that she hoped would get them moving. She explained that touch points were any interaction between the company and a customer, whether face-to-face, over the phone, on TV, or otherwise.

The team was quicker than they had been the previous day to identify activities through which the company made customer connections, things like marketing campaigns, the customer bill, and email correspondence. But as they charted the activities, two new collections of information began to surface. The first had to do with strengths and weaknesses.

"Sure, we do marketing campaigns," Arnie had said, "but we don't have good ways to measure conversion rates from various channels like the website or direct mail or even Twitter or Facebook. We're not all that sure what works better than others." This was important, Dana knew, but she was caught unprepared to manage it. So a new pair flip chart pages were started to collect the strengths and weaknesses.

The second set of information was about what touch point mattered most or rather how they would rank against each other in impact to the customer and the company. Melinda shared with the team that whenever new customers signed up because of a promotion like 50% off the first month or premium channels free for a month, they have a higher percentage of cancelling their entire subscription in the month after those promotions expired. She didn't have any data, but Melinda said they get a lot of calls in the service centers from customers who said they cancelled because they didn't realize how high the bill would be following the promotional period.

Arnie added, "Clearly, even marketing promotions can vary in impact among themselves. For example, we have excellent continuation rates from offering free high speed Internet access for a short time. Generally, when I think of touch points, I think of offers like this – where the customer is getting something new for free or at a reduced price – are going to be more impactful than, say, a regular bill we send to the customer. Since that bill is recurring, expected, and a bit administrative, it's typically pretty boring and doesn't carry a big impact. Clearly, not all touch points are created equal throughout a customer's lifecycle."

Dana thought immediately that this needed tracking, too. And they needed a system to rank the touch points and the types of things that happen at those touch points against their importance. Surely an upset customer with a billing question like Melinda was describing is more critical than helping someone find the channel guide on the website. Dana felt this might be important later on when they needed to prioritize, but she wasn't sure exactly yet how they would use it.

Again, more flip charts captured these as they surfaced, and again, Dana was left at day's end with a room full of paper and the need to generate spreadsheets to capture it all. The image of drowning in data flashed though her mind as she struggled to fold up and take home the dozen or so three-feet tall sheets of paper recording the day's work.

As she looked at all the information they were generating and wondered how best to organize it all, she realized this was not working smoothly. The team wasn't sure where they were going; indeed, she wasn't sure where they were going. The Customer Lifecycle Mapping and Touch Point Mapping exercises both sounded great when the conference speaker explained them. But the speaker had underplayed their complexity.

The woman who was known for "getting things done" was no longer as sure she could get this work done within the timeframes they'd been assigned. How would the team find their way through this? How would she?

TRUE
NORTH

It was Nick who suggested the call to Jane Friedman.
"Project beginnings can sometimes be a little rough,
Dana," Nick had tried to be reassuring, "but it sounds
like you're asking the right questions. You just have to
be careful you don't lose the team's confidence and coop-
eration as you look for the best ways to proceed.

"You're one of the best around here at putting out big
fires quickly. But we're committed to something different here – a strategic solution to customer relationships,
not just more one-offs. I wonder if your professor could
offer perspective? You've told me she's both taught this
customer experience strategy and helped companies de-

velop their own. Why don't you review the team's work with her and get her take?"

Dana had thought of this already, but there was that "prize student" part of her that didn't want her favorite professor to know she was stumbling. That was the downside of her initial decision to tell Jane and brag a little when the CEO had assigned her this new program.

I guess there's a time to eat crow, and a time to eat crow, she told herself, and made the call.

Jane listened intently as Dana admitted she was looking for some guidance. "How can I help?" she asked, and Dana described her sense that they were burying themselves with data. "Are we going to stall in analysis paralysis?" Dana asked.

"I doubt it," Jane began. "You did the most important thing absolutely correctly when you insisted on taking the customer's view. That's critical to a great customer experience. But you've started a journey, and you'll have a better chance of succeeding if you orient to True North, which is CableCorp's strategy and brand promise."

Jane wasn't finished. "A great customer experience doesn't just come from looking toward the brand promise. It comes from delivering on the brand promise consistently across all the touch points your team identified.

Let me remind you why this is so critical. Remember your dating days?"

Dating?

"You liked men who were more into you than they were into themselves, right?"

Dana agreed, thinking this actually wasn't a bad metaphor for the customer relationships they were trying to build. "So, where are you going with this?"

"Your potential 'keepers' were the ones who didn't just impress you at first, but rather ones that you were initially attracted to and who then displayed consistent personalities and behaviors over time," Jane reminded her. "Like relationships between people, relationships with companies are based on trust. And trust is built with consistent behavior over time."

Dana agreed. Sean wasn't the flashiest guy she'd ever dated, but it wasn't a roller coaster with him. If he said he'd call, he'd always call, even from the start. And his warmth and wit didn't disappear by the fourth date. It was consistency over time and the fact that he never pretended to be something he wasn't that won her for life. "Well, that and his parents' second home in the Caymans," Dana joked.

"I get it," Dana said. "A great customer experience

means our brand promise has been applied consistently to every customer interaction and stays that way over time. And you're saying my team needs to use the brand promises as the filter as we generate and plan against all this information."

"That's it," Jane confirmed.

Dana felt a little embarrassed now. "I've been trying to move the team away from thinking we're simply trying to help the CEO recover from the YouTube fiasco. That perspective is so ingrained it's hard to dislodge – it's even my default position, as you can see. I'm a brand pro, after all. How could I have missed the idea of starting with our strategy and brand promise?"

"Sometimes we miss things because they're just too close to us," Jane responded kindly. "But I'm betting that when your team clarifies what the company has really promised customers in the form of its brand, both the burning platform for this project and the best ways to organize the customer lifecycle and company touch points data will come more easily."

These were recommendations that Dana could move on. Strategy and branding, after all, were central to marketing, and she had endless amounts of information about this at her fingertips. Plus, she could easily pull big picture information on their competition; that would add energy and perspective to their brand understanding. And she could add examples of companies outside their industry who did customer experience really well – that might help keep the team's thinking focused on the project's end game. She'd get started on assembling these pieces right away. And she asked to check in with Jane one more time as a confirmation she'd gotten the plan right.

The check-in call was made Sunday night a few hours after she sent Jane an inbox-choking amount of material. Dana made sure to include the brand information and next steps. She outlined her intention to refresh the team's previous work using the brand as a guide. She also included her intentions to design the future customer experience.

"Well done, Dana," Jane responded. "But I have what may feel like bad news, too. I see you plan to refresh the data you've already collected against CableCorp's strategy and brand promise. Great. Then you plan to move on to a definition of the future state. There's actually one more step in the current state analysis that I think you'll greatly regret not taking, but it's a step you're not going to like."

"And the step is . . . ?"

"Business process mapping," Jane replied firmly.

"Process mapping? We're not doing re-engineering

here and I finally have the team focused on the customer side of things – now you want me to flip them back?" Dana protested.

"Ok." Educator-mode had taken over for Jane. "Each of these customer touch points you've identified is driven by a collection of CableCorp processes – that's how the company makes these touch points possible. Some of them are people processes; others are largely technology driven; most are a mix. Also, there are applications and data behind these processes. You need to uncover these and match them to the touch points they empower."

Dana was having a hard time hearing this. "Well, you'd make my IT guy delirious with joy if we included this in the work. His claim to fame is his process acumen. He'll envision a return to his former glory, and have us choking on spaghetti charts. I'm not resisting the wisdom of your thoughts here," she told Jane, "but pulling it off is something else . . ."

"Actually, I understand your hesitancy, and I don't think you're overestimating the challenge," Jane answered. "I just finished that large project with the insurance company, remember? I know that this step is essential. If you don't nail it early on, you'll find that when you come to the end, you will need to circle back and collect this data in order to make your recommendations substantial and credible. And doing it later is a slower, and even harder approach. Knock this out now – the other pieces ahead will come easier and make more sense once you have this completed. And I can send you a tool to help, something called a PAID diagram which stands for Process, Application, Integration, and Data."

"Jane, what would it take to get you to come and help us? To help me?" Dana asked. "I swear, the second time I lead a project like this, I'll be more confident, but I'm sailing a new ocean here, and we already determined that I started out with a compass not calibrated to True North.

"We don't have do-over time – and the risk to CableCorp is high enough on this one – that we can't do this project halfway," she concluded. "You've been through this many times before. Can you come and help me? If you'd facilitate the planning team sessions, and coach me on the side, I'm sure we can make this work."

The conversation had taken an unexpected direction. "Well, let me see," Jane responded, and agreed to confirm her teaching schedule while Dana began planning the case she'd take to Nick for additional funding. "With any luck," Dana said to Jane, "I'm about to get an amazing work partner."

*　　*　　*

Nick liked the idea of Jane's direct involvement, and agreed to use some of his own department budget to engage her. Meanwhile, Dana brought the team up to speed on the need to include a focus on strategy and brand.

However, this time Dana took a different approach. The professor had suggested a question. "So, instead of getting right to these branding documents," Dana began, "tell me this. What was your best all-time experience with a company as a customer? Who in your world really does this right?"

Their answers came quickly, much more quickly than some of the poster exercises she'd tried with them, Dana noted. And as they began to describe great experiences, she could feel energy building in the room.

Sharon described a local appliance store. Roger recalled a specialized power tool company that no one else was familiar with. Arnie rhapsodized about the sales and service at the BMW dealership. *Was it really that great?* Dana wondered, *or was this a chance to let them know his latest car purchase had been a Beamer?* Then she recalled the conference speaker who said some customers love companies and brands that "make them cool." His illustration was spot on, and he seemed newly engaged.

The investigation into "favorite brands" seemed to get the team to open up and think more clearly about moving CableCorp toward better customer interactions. Dana used this momentum to bring the conversation to their own brand. Now articulating and explaining the brand proved to be a practical exercise that gave direction.

Dana started to question deeper. "What was it about these companies and your interactions that made the customer experience so exceptional?" Dana asked the team. The answers were all across the board. The appliance store had a homey feel and served coffee and pastries; Sharon always felt welcome, like they were family. The tool catalog company always had the most inclusive inventory and obscure tool that Roger was seeking while being very easy to work with whenever it came to returns and exchanges. The BMW dealership made Arnie feel cool and important; it served as a status symbol for him, as if he was part of an elite group.

"So, we are saying that 'we make our customers' lives easier.' What exactly does that mean?" Dana questioned. The room was silent. Then Arnie spoke up, "It means we can package their media, Internet, and telephone services together on one bill." Dana nodded. Melinda said, "Well

I think it means when they call into our care centers that they actually talk to someone who has an answer and can provide that answer in a timely fashion."

Dana smiled, "Good." Then Roger quickly added, "It also means that we can actually get their billing correct so they don't have to call into the care center or their service doesn't go out so they don't have to wait for a tech to come visit."

Sharon then chimed it, "And if it does go out, maybe we should be able to fix things remotely or find better ways to quickly and painlessly make things right."

Dana continued to be pleased with the enthusiasm and participation in the room. "All of these responses can be correct," Dana proclaimed. "It is part of our effort to attain a level of detail and prescription surrounding what 'making our customers' lives easier' means. Or else, in the absence of a definition, our field associates will make up their own definition, and we'll be providing varying experiences that, while all well-intentioned, will be anything but consistent."

When they revisited their work on Customer Lifecycle Mapping, this time they added the company dimension as they mapped the processes and tools the company needed to support the customer experience.

Now, even the touch point mapping made more sense because they could more clearly see which touch points were critical. The recalibration of the data they'd already produced came more easily than she expected.

*　　*　　*

The following Monday, Dana had an introduction to make. "Team," she began, "I'd like you all to meet Jane." As it turned out, Jane needed little introduction. With a masterful and engaging story of her professional life, she had the whole team eating out of her hand. Dana then explained that she and Jane would take turns facilitating while the other captured and assimilated information on the fly. What she didn't share was that Jane would also be coaching Dana the rest of the way.

This new working arrangement and Jane's enthusiasm seemed to put the team into hyperdrive. Over the next week, their renewed focus and Jane's experience pushed progress through nearly all phases of the customer lifecycle. And Roger hadn't been blowing smoke about his abilities in process definition. He took a lead role in defining and mapping the underlying business processes at each customer activity. With Jane's tactful reminders and occasional cajoling, he even managed to keep them fairly high level.

"I guess the whole team doesn't need to get into every little detail," he said to Dana, with what she took to be his attempt to endorse her early comments.

Jane pushed them to identify the technical applications supporting each process, and then to map the data sources each drew from, using the tool she'd talked about earlier with Dana.

It was soon clear that subject matter experts from outside the team needed to join them, but Roger said he was on it and, over the next few days, they welcomed a member of the IT staff every couple of hours to learn about, and map, more applications and data sources. Roger kept the revolving door going and as the technologists came and went, the documentation grew and the list of issues within those processes and applications expanded. Dana was starting to see some clear burning platforms upon which she could build a case for a broad effort to redefine their customer experience.

Unfortunately, the addition of this process work had shifted their timeline for deliverables, but a status report to the senior team was still locked in for the following week.

"Can we push it out?" she asked Nick. "We're making progress, but we're just wrapping up documenting the current operations. We need to define our ideal experience and settle on the gaps before we'll have something the senior team can easily see as progress. If I were in their shoes, I'd wonder about how much time it's taking to come up with recommendations and whether their investment in developing this strategy was a good one."

Nick heard her out, but in the end decided it was more important to keep the status reporting schedule in place, so Dana delivered her update. This time Stuart didn't ask questions, but did grimace a bit as she closed with comments about the project expenses. Randall seemed even more engaged than when he first mandated the project's creation, and asked a couple of good questions about take-aways from the brand work.

Good to have his support, Dana thought to herself as she left the boardroom.

THE
ROADBLOCK

"Nobody should call you before 7:00 a.m.," Dana complained to Sean as she reached across the breakfast table for her phone. "Pre-caffeinated responses shouldn't count."

"At least not from you, that's for sure," Sean grinned.

It was Nick. This was early, even for him. "What's up?" Dana asked.

"It sounds like you haven't heard," Nick began.

"Heard what?"

"Randall. He was taken by ambulance to the hospital last night. Serious heart attack. He survived it, but reports this morning say they don't know the damage, won't know for several days, it looks like."

"Wow. That's terrible. I'll bet his family is scared to death," Dana exclaimed in an empathetic tone.

Nick replied, "I think everyone is taking it as well as can be expected, especially since Randall is stable, but he's going to need to relax for at least the next six weeks which will be followed by additional follow-up exams. I thought you would want to know. As for CableCorp, Stuart will be stepping in as acting CEO until a more definitive plan is created."

Dana was taken by surprise and her mind filled with thoughts of life being too short and what Randall's family must be going through. She told Sean what had happened. "My God, Sean. How terrible. Don't you ever put me through something like that. I don't think I could take it."

Sean replied in a way that was meant to lighten the situation. "Oh, honey, didn't I already commit to you years ago that I wouldn't die first?" The response elicited a brief grin from Dana, but not enough to pull her from her tragic thoughts. She slowly rose from the breakfast table and gave Sean a kiss goodbye. "I love you, honey," she reminded him, grabbed her keys and headed for the car.

During the morning she couldn't help but think about

Randall and his family. She knew she had to snap out of it and move forward. As the day progressed, her thoughts started to return to the project. Feeling selfish about even entertaining the question, she wondered if Randall's emergency would impact the program. *Stuart Betts leading the company?* Only her sense of good taste kept Dana from giving voice to the first question that sprang to her mind, but the question was clear: *What will happen to our project with Betts in the anchor chair, and more importantly, without Randall as its champion?*

Just before noon, Dana had another conversation with Nick. As if in response to her thoughts, Nick said, "We won't know for a while how much responsibility Betts will assume. His direction from the board right now is probably just to keep things running as usual and wait for more instructions as soon as more is known about Randall's condition. I'll keep you posted as we find out additional details, but I thought you'd want to tell the team."

She thanked him, glad that their understanding of each other had allowed them to not have to put self-serving questions on the table at this moment, but had also allowed each to acknowledge that this project they'd staked so much on could soon be in jeopardy.

No one on the team except Arnie had actually met

Randall, and a round of golf hardly counts as a personal friendship, no matter how hard Arnie tried to frame it. So they reacted as Dana expected, first with concern for Randall and his family and then with questions about the implications for the project.

"Right now nothing's changed," Dana assured them with more confidence than she felt. "Randall could spring back fairly quickly. We'll likely have Stuart Betts in place to guide the ship in the interim.

"In the meantime," she reminded them, "we have work to do and a delivery deadline that's not changed at all." Knowing that the team would not be human if these thoughts were not lingering in their minds during the day, Dana assumed progress on the day's task would difficult.

With that, Dana passed the meeting over to Jane who quickly moved them into what she called capability assessment work. Dana knew capabilities – it was what they'd always called the people, processes, and systems through which CableCorp delivered its services and the customer experience. But Jane was talking about something a little different here, and the assessment she was describing was going to be both large scale and a bit more tactical than their prior work.

The capabilities she presented were really bucketed

versions of the processes they'd identified back in the touch point mapping. Capabilities were her way of evaluating the business. Some were strategic, others operational, foundational or technical.

"The outcome of this work," she primed the team, "will be a clarified analysis of your business. It will define where you are today, where you stand against your competition, and where you want to be three years from now. Also, the work will provide an excellent foundation for identifying and defining the projects that will get you to where you want to be."

Jane already had a capability map ready to go – an organized set of 60 capabilities that included things like "Manage Billing," "Deliver Customer Service" and "Develop Campaigns." For each of the capabilities she had defined, they were going to do quick-and-dirty ratings right then and there. When Jane showed them the assessments they'd each be completing, Dana wondered if there'd be pushback from Roger about ball parking answers without backing them up with spreadsheets of data. And frankly, as she cut her teeth in the marketing research function, she had a bit of angst regarding the process, as well.

How did Jane know when to push them to dig for data, and when high-level answers would be better? *This was a skill she'd love to learn, Dana thought. Must have to do with experience.*

"I want you to give each capability a rating between zero and four," Jane instructed. "Zero means nothing's happening in this area; four is world class. We've talked about so many examples across a number of industries that I know you are aware of what world-class means. And you will be rating each capability on three components: How good is CableCorp now in this area? How good should CableCorp be? And how good is our competition?"

As soon as she outlined the questions, Dana felt relief at her decision to dive deeply into the customer lifecycle and the process mapping work Jane had recommended. This team had a solid understanding of the operations by now. They'd collected and hashed over the numbers and processes enough that by now, answering Jane's questions would result in pretty accurate and reasonable assessments. They weren't just going to be tossing darts at a dartboard.

The debate that followed confirmed Dana's hunch. Arm wrestling over whether their billing capability merited a one or three was supported by facts, along with knowledge of the investments other cable companies had made in upgrading their systems. They also knew from reviewing case studies what kinds of things leading customer experience companies were able to do. More often than not, people were speaking knowledgably about functions outside their own area and outside CableCorp's industry. Some real cross-functional perspective had developed.

The second part of Jane's exercise must point to another dimension, Dana thought. The team was asked to evaluate each capability against how important it was to customers, and also how important it was to the company. Another lively debate followed, but this time it was their grounding in strategy that seemed to guide the decision-making.

Dana found herself thinking that including this "importance" discussion was pure applied brilliance. Without it, they could wind up focusing their efforts on furthering business capabilities that were sorely immature, but which would matter little if, indeed, they didn't work perfectly.

Jane closed the day with an exercise she called "Imagine if. . ."

By now the team was more comfortable with challenges that looked playful on the surface, and had gotten fairly good at them. This one fit them well, because the outcome pointed directly to shaping the work for their final presentation. "Imagine if you had unlimited resources, no cap on spend or people, what would you do to improve each of the capabilities we've identified? What would CableCorp look like through the customer's eyes?"

"How about a customer calling for a replacement set top box, and it arrives not in days, but in say, 40 minutes – like a pizza delivery – but at no charge," Sharon suggested. Roger then added, "What if we could access the set top box remotely and diagnose the problem, or even fix it, without anyone needing to even go deliver that pizza."

"Or let's say a business customer's Internet connection goes down," Arnie jumped in, "but instead of the company saying *'Tough s***'*, we tell them a 4G device is being express mailed to them to keep them up and running while we fix the problem?"

This opportunity to create new possibilities engaged everyone, including the two newest team members, a pair from Finance who had just come on board to assist in preparation of the business cases ahead. Throughout the exercise, Jane had to remind them only once that they weren't thinking broadly or deeply enough. That quick reminder to stop fixing little pain points in their day-to-day operations and focus on true world-class capabilities, it was like flipping a switch.

The ideas grew bigger and grander and they started

coming faster. They were getting caught up in their own imaginations and enjoying it. Jane smiled across the room at Dana as if to say *they're getting it.* Of course, they all knew they wouldn't implement all of the ideas, but this daydream brainstorm was generating the kind of future-state ideas their strategy would need to leverage. *Tom Peters may be right after all in saying that employee innovation is the only competitive advantage,* Dana thought as she watched the team perform.

The ideas were only starting to slow down when Jane noted the time and decided to call it a day. She promised to return a readable version of their ideation session.

As soon as the team split up for the day, Jane and Dana huddled to go over their progress and talk about next steps. They'd move from the capability assessment, value mapping, and, of course, imagining the future to shaping and prioritizing projects. Jane asked Dana to develop a scorecard that, once they defined projects, could be used to capture the pertinent details and provide a single page view of the scope, some basic scoring about size and complexity, proposed solution, and how each project would push the needle in terms of value and capability maturity.

"Oh," she added, "and it's a good idea to always add a scenario, a story that paints a quick, but vivid picture of the end result – it makes it real and people can feel what it will be like." The work was really starting to get interesting now!

Dana realized it would take them right up to the deadline for the strategy project to assemble the information and analysis to generate the right projects in the right order, documented with scorecards and supported by high-level business cases. However, it looked far less impossible than it had a couple of weeks ago. Dana was glad she'd scheduled a meeting at day's end with Nick.

However, her one-on-one would not be all good news.

"Sit down, Dana," Nick said brusquely when she entered the room. Dana braced for the worst, considering the news from the morning.

"What's up?"

"I have some bad news."

"Randall Phillips?" Dana said quickly. "I thought he was out of the woods. Recovering slowly, but recovering."

"Oh, sorry, I didn't mean to worry you – you heard that right," Nick said. "But I've just left a meeting of the senior team. Looks like Phillips won't be back for months... maybe longer." Dana was actually relieved by the news. Her first reaction to "bad news" was that perhaps Randall's condition had deteriorated.

Nick continued. "So the board has expanded Stuart's authority, charged him with more than just holding the status quo. He's to go ahead and run the company until Phillips is ready to take the helm again."

"Wow, Stuart Betts in the CEO's chair for longer?" Dana coughed. "We'll be told to steal ballpoint pens from hotels to keep office supply expenses down."

"This isn't a joke," Nick looked at her soberly. "And I've mentioned before that he's a sound leader of this organization and we are lucky to have him watch over the finances as he has. But we may also need to adjust to his guidance which may include the customer experience project. As his first act of leadership, he's calling for a review of all projects he calls 'exploratory.'

"I don't think Stuart intends to turn the place upside down, but rather to get a better handle on what's going on and maybe move things forward in a way that he knows best. There will certainly be a focus on the basics." Nick went on, almost to himself. "It's the drum he's been beating at our staff meetings since the beginning."

Dana looked at him. "So how does that affect us? I didn't exactly think of our project as exploratory; Randall rather called it an imperative and put his personal stamp on it."

"You haven't been listening," Nick chided her. "Betts is now in charge, and our project is not out of the ideation phase which makes it exploratory. Our project," he paused to be sure she was paying attention, "is second on his review list."

The impact of what Nick was saying got through. "He was reluctantly supportive of our work from the start," Dana said, though she knew this was obvious to both of them. "So that just makes it that much more important to speak his language in the project review," Nick finished her sentence, "We need to make such an airtight case for the ROI of this work that it would be foolish not to move forward."

"Whoa. The world just shifted in a big way," Dana said. "We have a lot more work to do in the next month – and it's going to have to be even more detailed than what I was anticipating."

"You must have missed it," Nick shook his head. "You heard right about the need for an irrefutable business case justification, but your review date isn't a month out. It's been moved up to eight days from now."

You could see the color run from Dana's face. "Did you say eight days?" Dana said slowly, as if the words didn't make sense. "You and I both know that's impossible!

We've got projects to frame and justify, and scorecards and business cases to create. And a roadmap to design. We've just started into the really time-consuming stuff."

"You can swear and scream," Nick told her, more gently now. "I did my version of both, and all it got us was a couple of extra days. Stuart had initially scheduled you for *five* days from now, but after my protests, the Consumer Markets president took pity and offered to trade his review time for ours. From that we got the weekend plus a couple of days. It's rotten, I know, but it's as good as I could do."

There was little more to discuss so Dana thanked Nick for the update and headed pensively toward the elevator.

If Stuart could see numerically what she was coming to see intuitively from their work, this would be an initiative even he could support. However, intuition doesn't sell multi-million dollar programs. Data and financials do that. Besides, they'd be appearing before the court of Judge Betts, guilty until proven innocent. The burden of proof was on her team and the judge wasn't going to be sympathetic.

Dana Chase, Queen of "Git 'er done" had just been dealt an impossible hand.

THE
DECISION

The team exploded when Dana shared Nick's news, a clear sign to Dana that they were now as invested in this outcome as she was. And they echoed her angst, though in stronger terms.

Leadership required you walk a fine line, Dana reminded herself. She represented this company, after all, and there was a way in which she needed to soldier on. Her team deserved to know they had a talented executive team and that there was hope they would be successful. But honesty had to be in the mix, too. It's what she appreciated most about Nick – he had the strength to keep from blaming others when things didn't work, but he never insulted her with company-speak that she knew was prescribed by someone higher up.

"I know that what we are doing is what will make this company better. Will make it possible to achieve its vision, its brand promises. But we have an uphill battle to make our point and allow others to see how important this is for CableCorp. What we're doing has not been done in the history of the projects here. With that novelty comes resistance, unless we are able to provide hard reasons to keep going. Right now, I feel it's one shot for us," she told the team. "It's really a go or no go decision eight days from now, and it will determine the fate of this work and certainly the direction of the company. I don't expect we'll get a second chance."

The team was quiet for a moment. Melinda broke the silence. "Then I say we kick ass and take names." Her ferocity was so out of character, but on-the mark, that everyone laughed and Dana could see the resolution return to their faces.

"Okay," Arnie said, as if he'd been appointed spokesperson, "we better break this down and figure out what we have to do. The clock is ticking."

Jane jumped in and started to lay out what they needed to do to fast track the remaining work. As it turned out, there were a number of things they could shorten and a few other shortcuts they could take to save some time.

The work was fairly straightforward: identify initiatives and bucket them into meaningful categories. Develop business cases – that meant working on estimating costs, articulating benefits, and setting time expectations.

The team showed some slight panic when she talked about the business cases, but she assured them they had everything they needed and that these would be "strategy-level" business cases – in other words, high level, but still relevant. Then, scorecards would describe each project in summary form and a roadmap would show how it all would come together.

Nick provided them with a couple of key pieces of advice that proved particularly useful. "Be careful with your metrics," he told them. "Large-scale projects like this tend to draw from business unit metrics that fit project-by-project, but don't translate well into the metrics we use company-wide to measure profitability. Unless the senior team can quickly see these familiar metrics, they may not realize soon enough the amount of impact your overall roadmap of projects can have.

"Gear your scorecards to the key quantitative financials for the company, like gross adds, cost per gross add, revenue per subscriber, churn, and operating expenses. When you work through revenue, don't forget to classify it like we report to the street: Video, Internet, Telephone, Commercial, and Ad Sales – although in this strategy, I doubt you'll have much for that last one. While metrics like customer satisfaction, net promoter score, loyalty, and customer ease are important indicators of customer sentiment, what this team, and Stuart in particular, will be looking for are estimated project costs against revenue, operational cost savings or increases, and the net effect to the bottom line. You know what I'm talking about."

Actually, some on the team didn't. But at this point, their decision to expand the team to include Finance proved to be even wiser than they'd expected. These two knew the metrics backwards and forwards, knew how to dig under the company's long-term projections, and had excellent recommendations for measures that fit the project categories. And they were fast! Financial projections that would have taken days to gather without their help turned up in a couple of hours.

An unexpected source of support came from Dana's boss Alex, the chief marketing officer. Up until now, Alex had been almost a shadow figure in Dana's work, appearing at staff meetings and performance reviews, but not much else. She'd only had a few interactions with him, but not much coaching.

He called it a "hands-off management style" but Dana read it as disinterest even though she knew setting up reviews was in large part on her. So when Dana got the call to meet with him, she was more frustrated than curious. *Now? Like I have time for this when so much is at stake?* She tried to reschedule with Alex's assistant, but the assistant made it clear the appointment was locked in.

As it turned out, Alex had an offer of help. "I know you've given this your best shot, Dana," he began. *And he would know this how?* Dana thought. But she said nothing.

"But here's something I think could make a difference. You've made no connections with senior team members about the project – no interviews, no updates, no reviews. The meeting will go much better if you give the executive team an opportunity to preview the presentation.

"I'd suggest you and Nick do a walk-around. Take your presentation deck and meet one-on-one with each exec who will be at the table with Stuart. Show them what you'll call your 'provisionary recommendations' and get their reaction. Ask for their input or even their advice. You may end up not getting any help, or even support, but you may be surprised. And at least you'll be better prepared for what to expect when you walk into that boardroom. At the very least, you'll know where to turn for support during the presentation, and where your challengers will come from."

Dana had to admit it was good advice. Self-reliance served her well most of the time. It was largely this quality that had earned her the "Git 'er done" tag. But Alex had identified a real miss. The project needed these people. Their strategy would impact the departments they led. She'd talk with Nick about game planning a bit, as well as making sure he could join her in the meetings.

* * *

In the end, talking with the executives proved more productive than she expected. Dana realized some of the team's work could have gone more smoothly if she'd checked in earlier. Overall, they asked good questions, and two gave ideas neither she nor Nick had considered regarding how to frame parts of the final presentation. A couple, however, seemed unsold on the whole idea, but that was where Nick stepped up and asked some good questions to get at exactly where their concerns were. In each meeting, the end result was a set of good recommendations and what felt like growing support.

It was clear to Dana that she was cashing in on the smart and supportive way Nick had participated at the senior table in the last few months. These people wanted to help as much as they could without putting their own functions at risk. "Good learning," Dana thought. "I'll approach executive alignment differently in the future."

It was Nick who came up with the solution to their big problem. The proposal was coming down to a design for 12 projects over two years, with the help of over 100 people. A spend of nearly $80 million. The magnitude of it caught the whole team by surprise. How would they talk about this without getting laughed out of the room?

"You guys have to show quick wins," he reminded them. "You are predicting overall bottom-line benefits in the range of $500 million over the lifetime of the business cases; certainly a return like that makes an investment like this worth it. And the assumptions that led to the numbers look good – don't forget how conservative we were along the way. We are far from stretching our necks out on most of this. But you've got to show results faster than two years, or the low risk players in the room won't sign on. Heck, even the risk tolerant will probably lose interest after 12 months and start to find new ways to spend the money."

Dana noted he didn't mention Stuart or his position, though they all knew which camp he would be in. It's that "good soldier" thing used the right way, she noted.

"What do we have that we could pull from the roadmap and do right away? Something that shows good return that we can turn around first, in maybe three months or so. Maybe it's a preview version that delivers some results while we continue to work on the big bang. We need something that may buy us time to work on the stronger-returning initiatives that will take time to implement."

This made good sense and Dana also noted Nick's use of "we" and "us" more and more. After a quick discussion, they decided to spend the afternoon identifying half a dozen "quick win" initiatives they could launch almost immediately after getting approval – if it came. In the end, they settled on three that would set the stage nicely for some later efforts while still delivering benefits. Everyone agreed that they could be implemented in three or four months. These "quick wins" were the final piece as their proposal came together.

The night before her presentation, the team went out to dinner. "The Last Meal of the Condemned," Roger had drolly labeled it, but their mood was surprisingly light. They knew their work was solid. It supported everything they had wanted to do for customers while showing a very strong return. The presentation would be a challenge, no doubt, but it was the right thing to propose and the right thing to do for the company and its customers.

The bittersweet part of the evening came with a video Arnie and Sharon had created, a remake of the YouTube piece that had started it all, but this time with a giddy customer lauding the turnaround in CableCorp's services. They'd planned initially to show it as part of the presentation to the senior team. Now that idea didn't fit, so they chose to just enjoy it together. At the end, Arnie and Sharon added a surprise – a short video montage of the team working together. They thought back to all the working lunches, funny jokes, tense moments, outright arguments, and some occasional hugs that were shared along the way.

As they left the restaurant, the team agreed to meet in their planning room while Dana presented, with the expectation that no matter the outcome, they'd get a blow-by-blow right after. "We're going to finish this thing together," Melinda said, and all agreed.

*　　*　　*

The next morning, Dana walked out of the boardroom with a mixture of emotions. She thought she'd mentally played out all the options, and how she'd deal with each, but this one…it hit her blindside.

The presentation went as planned, no surprises there. And the grilling that followed, well, few surprises there, either. Stuart was as tough and poised to strike as she expected, and as knowledgably interrogative as she thought he would be.

Nick had prepared her well. He'd coached her to relax. "You don't need to be defensive," he told her. "Your team has done a spectacular job. Some things you can control; some you can't. You'll love work over the long haul if you remember which are which, and only worry about the ones you control. Stuart isn't one of those."

She agreed, and once again gave thanks for his wisdom. With this mindset, she felt surprisingly calm when responding to Stuart's questions. And she found that a couple of others at the table stepped in with supportive information when she stumbled. Who'd have expected it, especially when Dr. No would soon be calling for reviews of their projects?

"When it was done," she related to her team, "we didn't get the approval we wanted, but we didn't get rejected either."

"What are you talking about?" Sharon asked.

"He called it a 'provisional approval,' Dana explained. No need to say which 'he' she was referencing; they all knew. "The case was so compelling, and your work in painting a credible picture of the possibilities was so well done, that Stuart thought it foolish not to continue. So he gave the green light to the quick wins. We have six months to make them work – implementation through measuring results, and then a readout with the senior team before they decide on the long-term strategy.

"So, congratulations . . . ," she smiled. "It appears we have a project. And since I know we didn't over-promise on the quick hits, I believe we also have a program. The challenge is going to be keeping the roadmap intact because we don't have the funding to start any long term projects while the quick wins are being delivered, but I think we can do it, with some juggling and perhaps a little hit to our overall business case."

"Then it's time for your gift," Melinda announced, and handed her a deep blue, nicely-bound book. "It's from all of us, the book we think the company needs most right now. And besides this copy, we've also sent a copy to Stuart."

When she saw the title, Dana burst out laughing. In bold letters it read, "The Chase for Excellence in Customer Experience."

"You sent this to Stuart Betts?"

"Ah, just kidding about that," Melinda smiled. The book itself, however, was filled with blank pages.

"We made sure the pages were empty," Melinda explained, "because this is a story we'd like to write together."

"Count on it," Dana said. "Absolutely. Count on it."

THE
RETURN

Randall Phillips stood and stretched out a hand in greeting as Dana entered the room. "How was your flight?" he asked as she took off her coat.

"Good, quick," she responded. "LaGuardia beats JFK anytime for an easy connection to downtown." Randall looked rested, Dana noted. Though the initial recovery from his heart attack had taken a full six months, he'd since been serious about taking his doctors' advice on changes in his lifestyle, and the results were evident.

"By the way," Randall added, "My assistant told me this morning as her factoid of the day that it was exactly three years ago today that we first met in my office to talk about a customer service intervention."

"Now that's what I call an assistant with attention to detail!" Dana said jokingly. "But really, when I think back to how much I underestimated what it takes to make big changes happen in a company like ours, I'm humbled. Does accepting your offer to lead small stuff always wind up with people in over their heads for a couple of years?" Dana inquired.

He laughed with her. "Not always. But I seem to have pretty good skills at picking the ones to load up. You knocked the ball out of the park with this Customer Experience work, Dana. And it's more than just the profitability we're now enjoying. What people say about our company is what I hoped they'd be saying when I became a CEO."

"That's pretty powerful stuff," Dana agreed. "Thank you."

Just then their conversation was interrupted by a woman with a clipboard wearing a headset. "Are you two ready?" she asked with a smile. "We are about to go to commercial, then you're on."

As they rose to follow her out of the Green Room, the show's host could be heard from the TV monitor above them.

"It's been some time since CableCorp CEO Randall

Phillips was on our show in the aftermath of the now classically famous 'My Kids Hate CableCorp' YouTube video.

"After the break, he'll join us to talk about his company's dramatic turnaround in top line revenue growth, customer satisfaction and reduction in subscriber loss. And he's brought along Dana Chase, the CableCorp VP that Phillips credits with engineering the changes that led to the turnaround. We'll be right back…"

As they walked onto the set, Randall Phillips leaned over to Dana. "Just one more thing, Ms. Chase. What are we going to do about Netflix?"

THE
APPROACH
TO CUSTOMER
EXPERIENCE
STRATEGY

ANDREW REISE CONSULTING

Our Customer Experience Journey

In 2004, Andrew Reise Consulting was founded based on the premise that consulting could be done a better way. Specifically, we set out to enhance the client experience – partnering with clients as opposed to pushing our own agendas. We always seek to exceed expectations as opposed to meeting contractual commitments, and build meaningful relationships as opposed to sealing the deal and moving on to the next one. Our approach to client service and our expertise in delivering CRM solutions has evolved into a passion for helping clients with their own customer experience challenges. In other words, we founded our firm on the core principles of delivering a better customer experience.

As the book portrays, we often see companies make significant investments in "one off," disconnected initiatives in an attempt to improve their customer experience. Oftentimes, they embark on this journey before they have a clear vision of where they are going, resulting in a return on investment that is never realized. We decided to write this book to share some of our key learnings with the hope they will benefit business leaders embarking on their own customer experience journeys and help companies thrive in the process.

As you may have experienced on your own, and as the book points out, creating and sustaining the desired customer experience can be very tricky indeed. As with any complex program, you'll likely encounter some surprises along the way. We hope that these tools and techniques will aid you in your journey and serve as a guide in your own customer experience adventures.

How We View Customer Experience

We view customer experience as one continuous end-to-end process. Like any process, the customer experience process can work perfectly (or go horribly wrong), include hundreds of touch points, and can be analyzed, re-engineered, and optimized. The customer experience process does not begin and end at your store, sales representative, website, or call center. It extends from the moment the customer becomes aware of your company and lasts until they stop using your products or services. Simply put, the customer experience process is broad, deep, iterative, and (hopefully) long running.

The good news is that you have the opportunity to positively shape the customer's experience with every interaction. The bad news is that every interaction must be consistent, across all channels, and match your brand promise in order to build trust and confidence with your customers. As Professor Jane in the story reminds us, relationships that customers have with companies are like relationships they have with people. They are based upon trust, and the best way to build trust is through consistent behavior over time. As simple as this may sound, it is very challenging for companies to create, implement and sustain a superior customer experience that develops the trust that is essential in developing loyal customers.

Our methodology uses an "outside-in" approach when looking at the customer and company relationship (Figure 1). This allows us to design and optimize the customer experience from the customer's point of view. Looking 'outside' first, we seek to gain insights into the customer's needs, wants and expectations. We then look 'inside' to establish a clear understanding of the company's brand and strategic vision. Where these two sides meet are the various touch points that marry customer needs and wants with the company's products and services. Our experience has shown that most companies struggle with designing and managing business capabilities that will deliver the brand promise at every touch point every time.

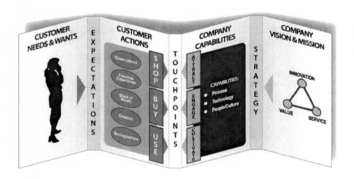

Through our experience, we have identified four key principles that are critical to creating and sustaining the right customer experience strategy and capabilities for your company.

Principle #1. Align the Experience with Your Corporate and Brand Strategy

A company's customer experience must align with the organization's overarching corporate strategy. Companies such as Apple (innovator), Wal-Mart (low-prices), or Ritz Carlton (luxury) each have a clear and unique corporate strategy and brand. Customer perceptions and expectations will clearly be different for each one of these strategies. Therefore, it is crucial to have a clearly defined brand that is constantly taken into consideration when designing the capabilities to support your customer experience strategy. The goal is to design an experience for your customers that is consistent across all customer touch points and effectively delivers your brand promise.

Principle #2. Understand the Customer

In order to truly understand your customer's experience when interacting with your company, you must look at it from the customer's perspective. This is particularly helpful when going through customer scenario and lifecycle mapping. You will find that different pain points and opportunities arise when looking at things from the customer's viewpoint as opposed to your company's perspective.

Think about what the customer expects as they SHOP, BUY and USE your company's products or services. How might the customer feel? Is the experience complicated or simple? Did the company deliver on its brand promise?

In order to understand the needs, wants and expectations of your customer, you need to listen. Voice of the Customer data can come from a variety of sources, including transactional surveys, focus groups, customer analytics tools, social media sites, and even customer escalations to executives. Analyzing, understanding, and utilizing the true voice of your customer is a key component to the development and continuous improvement of your customer experience strategy.

Principle #3. Deliver the Brand Promise Through Touch Points

Touch points are where the customer and the brand promise meet. It is where the rubber meets the road. While each touch point is important, its role in the customer experience lifecycle can only be truly understood by putting it into the context of the customer's point of view. It is important to map out ALL customer touch points and group them into scenarios that comprise the ideal customer experience. For example, an advertisement may appear to be just fine to the company. But it can be downright frustrating for a customer that watches the TV advertisement, reads a review on Angie's List, and is unable to order the item at the stated price.

In order to be successful, you must also understand how all touch points are delivered and how they may enhance or detract from the brand's perception. Not only do your employees leave lasting impressions on your customers, but so do vendor partners, big box retailers, bloggers, franchisees, and anyone else that is associated with your brand. You may not be able to control all of these touch points, but you can certainly influence them. In order to do that, you must first understand the broad reaching scope of touch points that comprise your customer experience. Then work to determine which ones may be falling short of your brand promise.

Principle #4. Business Capabilities Deliver the Experience

If each touch point is a stage, then business capabilities are the props, special effects, and acts that get performed on the stage. Business capabilities consist of people, process and technology. All must work in concert and be aligned to the overarching corporate strategy.

You can have the best employees on the planet, but if they don't have customer centric business capabilities to support them, the customer experience will suffer. Conversely, even the best of process or technology capabilities won't improve the customer experience if front-line employees don't use them effectively or aren't empowered.

When evaluating your business capabilities, you must look at them holistically to determine dependencies across people, process, and technology dimensions as well as across all channels.

Furthermore, don't assume that just because your company may have a certain capability that you do it well. As with most things in life, capabilities change. The online website capabilities that were launched back in 1998 are, well, so last century. The bar for each capability seems to rise each and every year. That is why we recommend evaluating each capability's relative maturity level compared to the state of the industry and key competitors. By doing so, companies can better gauge where they stand, identify where they need to improve, and establish a model for continuous improvement.

How to Create Your Customer Experience Strategy

We recognize that each company is unique and there is no 'one size fits all' approach to customer experience. Based on our experience, however, we've developed a straightforward framework that can help almost any company as they embark on their customer experience journey.

Our framework begins with a healthy assessment of your brand and your customers, digs into the details of the touch points and associated capabilities that comprise the customer experience, and concludes with the identification of valuable and pragmatic projects that comprise a customer experience roadmap tailored to your company.

Step 1: Analyze Your Brand Promise

It is critical that everyone on the strategy team has a clear understanding of the company's brand promise and how it is differentiated from the competition. This helps to lay the foundation that is so critical throughout the entire customer experience strategy development process.

Key Activities

- Analyze company culture and brand documentation to ensure a clear understanding of corporate strategy. Are you competing on product, service or price?
- Define your True North – develop clear project vision and mission statements
- Conduct competitor analysis – Conduct an analysis of what customer experience capabilities are

being delivered by key competitors

- Leverage research and best practices for companies known for their customer experience

Results

- Project team alignment and understanding of corporate brand promise
- Clear direction on what the team has set out to accomplish
- Initial ideas on how to enhance your customer experience

Tip: Don't attempt to reinvent your brand promise; Instead, seek to understand what the company, as well as customers, perceive to be the brand promise.

Step 2: Listen to the Voice of the Customer

Gain customer insight by understanding customer needs, wants, expectations, and influencers. Gather any available customer information to analyze behaviors, trends, common themes, and root causes. These insights will help to guide the design of specific customer experiences and provide credibility to your strategic recommendations.

Key Activities

- Gain access to internal customer data (i.e., transactional surveys, segmentation analysis, social media feedback, speech analytics, focus groups, etc.)
- Analyze customer data to identify key themes, preferences, and opportunity areas
- Create a customer needs network based on holistic needs and wants

Results

- Overall "voice of the customer" for your company
- Insights into customer needs, wants, and preferences
- Understanding of key customer metrics to be used for measurement / business case

Tip: It is incredibly difficult to design the right customer experience if you don't know what the customer wants. Dig into available data to learn what makes your customers tick.

Step 3: Map the Customer Lifecycle

Mapping the customer experience lifecycle is an important first step to establishing an end-to-end process model. This model helps to galvanize the team to take a customer-centric viewpoint and serves as the foundation for which touch points and business capabilities can be evaluated. Additionally, mapping the lifecycle will allow you to 'connect the dots' of the broader customer experience ecosystem.

Key Activities

- Assemble a cross functional team to define customer lifecycle phases and subsequent customer experience activities
- Document 'as is' process steps for each phase and identify issues or gaps

Results

- Detailed Customer Lifecycle map
- Current state documented and understood by all stakeholders
- Clearly documented and understood pain points, issues and brand gaps

Tip: Make sure to look at the experience from the customer's viewpoint when mapping the customer lifecycle. This will identify new opportunity areas that would not be discovered if viewing it from the company's perspective.

Step 4: Create and Analyze PAID Diagrams

The nuances of delivering great end-to-end customer experience lies in the details. Unravel the complexities of how different people, process, and technology capabilities enable the customer experience by creating a PAID (Process, Application, Integration, and Data) diagram. A PAID diagram directly maps how the various components of the ecosystems contribute to the overall customer experience.

Key Activities

- Assemble cross functional team of business stakeholders and IT/application owners to create PAID diagrams via collaborative workshops
- Identify how people, process, and technology capabilities enable or detract from the customer experience

Results

- Documented PAID diagrams that align all people, process, and technology capabilities to the end-to-end customer experience
- Gaps between the ideal customer experience and current capabilities

Tip: The true value of PAID diagrams lies in the journey rather than the destination. Unify the diverse group of indi-

viduals and capabilities that comprise the typically complex customer experience ecosystem by collaborating in the creation of a common PAID diagram.

Step 5: Explore the Ecosystem of Customer Touch Points

To properly understand the customer experience ecosystem, inventory the customer touch points that a customer may encounter during the lifecycle of the customer experience. Then analyze the relationships between touch points by modeling customer scenarios that represent the various ways that customers may navigate your touch points.

Key Activities

- Inventory all touch points that comprise the customer experience ecosystem
- Analyze the relationship between touch points by utilizing scenarios
- Validate the customer experience ecosystem with employees, partners and customers

Results

- Quantifiable view of the customer experience ecosystem.

- Clear view of how individual components of the ecosystem influence the customer experience

Tip: Individual touch points, although important, don't tell the entire story. Explore the customer experience ecosystem by identifying all possible touch points and analyzing their inter-relationships through various scenarios.

Step 6: Assess Capability Maturity

In order to effectively improve capabilities, companies must be able to gauge where and to what degree they need to improve, and establish a model for continuous improvement. This is done by evaluating the current business capabilities that enable the customer experience by assigning a relative maturity score based on a 5-point scale. Each capability's maturity level can then be compared to the target maturity level as well as the perceived maturity levels of the industry and key competitors.

Key Activities

- Conduct an assessment of all capabilities that enable the customer experience
- For each capability, assign a maturity score for your current state, desired future state, and per-

ceived industry and competitors offerings

- Conduct a gap analysis to determine the greatest needs for improvement

Results

- Understanding of your organization's "capability health" and desired future state
- Ideas and opportunity areas for improvement

Tip: Don't assume that all capabilities should target the highest maturity level. Instead, pick the subset of capabilities that best align with your corporate and brand strategy and focus your efforts there.

Step 7: Identify The Portfolio of Projects

Aggregate the various recommendations and initiatives from the previous steps into a portfolio of customer experience projects. Reinforce the interdependencies between projects and consider other enterprise initiatives or programs that are teed up or in flight.

Key Activities

- Analyze the output from previous steps to create a list of tactical projects
- Rationalize and group common projects into initiatives

- Conduct high level estimate (High, Medium, Low) of resources, budget and timeline for each initiative
- Determine value drivers, key metrics and high level business benefit for each initiative
- Prioritize projects based on business need and/or value contribution (business need may be either revenue generation, cost reduction, or both)

Results

- Prioritized list of initiatives that can be implemented to improve overall customer experience
- High level cost/benefit analysis for each initiative

Tip: Divide your customer experience transformation into manageable pieces to allow for stepwise or iterative improvements.

Step 8: Develop the Customer Experience Business Case

The ultimate goal of improving your customer experience is to improve business results and financial outcomes for the company. In order to do so, you must have a solid business case that shows the relationship between strategic recommendations and key business metrics. Develop a formal customer experience business case that links the projects and/or activities to specific customer value drivers. Include both quantitative and qualitative benefits to be achieved by the project.

Key Activities
- Develop a detailed business case for all or sub set of high priority projects
- Review with key stakeholders and functional leaders

Results
- Detailed cost, benefit and timeline estimate that will be used to secure program funding/approval

Tip: An effective customer experience business case must link the art of customer experience with the science of traditional financial metrics such as revenue, expense, profit, and cash flow.

Step 9: Create Roadmap and Present to Executives

Creating a comprehensive program roadmap can help serve as a long range guide to your efforts. Start by assembling and sequencing projects that depict the customer experience journey and clearly shows the path to achieving your customer experience goals. Highlight the phases, activities, resources, and milestones necessary to take customer experience initiatives from inception to reality.

Key Activities

- Arrange and group projects into initiatives or programs
- Taking timeline, risks and dependencies into consideration, create an implementation roadmap that includes a high level timeline, phases, and key milestones
- Determine organization needs required to deliver the roadmap
- Create an executive presentation that outlines the clear problem statement or burning platform, highlights key findings, clearly articulates the need to implement the roadmap, and quantifies financial benefits

Results

- Customer Experience Roadmap
- Executive Presentation

Tip: *Bring the roadmap to life. Create a visual overview of the phases and activities required to complete your customer experience project.*

Additional Resources

For more information about our customer experience strategy development framework, visit us online at *www.AndrewReise.com.*

Andrew Reise

C O N S U L T I N G

www.AndrewReise.com

Andrew Reise helps companies with Customer Experience strategy and implementation.

<u>Core Offerings</u>

Experience Assessments   We provide clients with an understanding of key Customer Experience principles and their maturity level against those principles.

Strategy Development   Our framework is robust, yet flexible and encompasses best practices and proven tools to create your Customer Experience roadmap that is in-line with your brand and overall business strategy.

Business Enablement and Leadership   Andrew Reise consultants are seasoned, delivery experts that use proven program management practices and leadership to implement your Customer Experience vision.

Customer Insights   We help clients make sense of their customer data by conducting detailed analysis, developing business cases and implementing tactical plans that deliver results.

Go to www.AndrewReise.com to download the top pitfalls of Customer Experience Transformations and how to avoid them.

CPSIA information can be obtained at www.ICGtesting.com
Printed in the USA
LVOW13*2000150114

369606LV00001B/2/P